D0462499

Word Whiz's
Guide to

California
Middle School
Vocabulary

By Chris Kensler

A Paper Airplane Project

New Yo~~rk~~   Toronto

Kaplan Publishing
Published by Simon & Schuster, Inc.
1230 Avenue of the Americas
New York, NY 10020

For bulk sales to schools, colleges, and universities, please contact: Order Department,
Simon & Schuster, 100 Front Street, Riverside, NJ 08075. Phone: 1-800-223-2336. Fax:
1-800-943-9831.

Cover Design: Cheung Tai
Interior Page Design and Production: Paper Airplane Projects

Manufactured in the United States of America

September 2001

10 9 8 7 6 5 4 3 2 1

Library of Congress Cataloging-in-Publication Data

ISBN 0-7432-1104-9

All of the practice questions in this book were created by the authors to illustrate question types. They are not actual test questions.

Table of Contents

About the Author

Chris Kensler grew up in Indiana and attended Indiana University, where he majored in English. He has edited several test prep publications, worked as feature writer/reporter for a daytime drama publication, and written a book or two, including *Study Smart Junior*, which received the Parents' Choice Award. Currently, he is the editor of an art magazine, is married to the lovely woman who designed this book, and has some cool cats and a dog named Joe.

Les Angeles is a figment of his imagination.

Acknowledgments

The author would like to thank Maureen McMahon, Lori DeGeorge, and Beth Grupper for their help in shaping and editing the manuscript, and Chris Dreyer for copyediting this book.

The publisher wishes to thank Melanie Meredith for her contributions to this book.

Dedication

For Louise Sebene.

Introduction

Hi. My name is Les. Les Angeles. I'm here
to help you with your vocabulary.

As you can probably tell from my name, I'm from California. I'm in the eighth grade, and at my school I'm famous for two things—my board and my vocabulary. Like my idol Corky Carroll, I've been surfing since I was a little kid. Every day, I taste some tasty waves. At one point, I had surfed 234 days in a row, a record among my friends. Surfing's just like anything else: the more you do it, the better you get. In fact, with the amount of time I've put in and the trophies I've won, I could probably go pro if I wanted to. But school's too important for me to do that.

See, I take school pretty seriously. I have improved my vocabulary by practicing, too. By reading books, writing essays and stories, and by just generally paying attention to words in everyday life. All that practice has turned me into a Word Whiz. Now I'm going to turn you into one.

If you're having trouble on tests, one reason might be because you are having trouble understanding the words. Of course, the first and most likely reason you blank or panic or freak out on tests is that instead of studying, you keep watching your new *Chicken Run* DVD. Still, sometimes things don't go so well even when you do study. That's the worst. You're like, dude, I studied all night and I still got a D! What's up with that?

Sometimes it's because you just aren't comfortable with the words on the test. For example, say you are taking a math test and one of the questions asks you to find the "perimeter of a rectangle." It's not hard to do—you just add up all the sides. But if you space out on what the word "perimeter" means, you're in trouble. Your brain freezes. Does it have something to do with periscopes? Or maybe something to do with meters? The next thing you know, you have a picture of a submarine doing the 40-meter dash in your head. Not cool.

Believe me, I've been there. It's no fun. But it doesn't have to be that way.

Word Whiz Is Here to Help

Believe it or not, you probably already know more than 10,000 words total. It just happens. The older you get, the more words get added to your vocabulary. But let's not talk about the words you already know, let's focus on the words you need to know. The 600 words in this book are the most important ones to know for middle school homework and

tests. I call them WhizWords. If you know these WhizWords backward and forward, you will be in good shape at school, and you will no doubt become rich and successful when you grow up.

I'm going to review these WhizWords for you by relating them to things you're probably interested in, like TV, movies, sports, music, celebrities, and the stuff kids like us like to do when we're NOT in school. All these things can help you learn these words.

I'm also going to explain them to you in words you already know. The problem with a lot of dictionaries is the words they use in the definition are harder than the word they are defining! Or they just repeat the word. Here's an example—the definition of "impartial" from a popular dictionary (I won't name names):

impartial—adj. not partial; unprejudiced.

Gee, thanks a lot! Believe me, if I knew what "partial" meant, I could probably figure out impartial. And "unprejudiced?" How many syllables is that? Eleven? Geez. And of course they don't give a sample sentence. Now here's my definition:

impartial—adj. fair. Judges and juries are supposed to be <u>impartial</u>. That means they just go by the facts. Like Judge Judy on TV—she is an <u>impartial</u> judge who listens to all the facts, then she reams the person who is guilty.

Better, right? I'm also only going to give you the one or two meanings that you are most likely to see on a test or in class. Some words have tons of different meanings, and regular dictionaries have to list them all. But in my book, I am just going to focus on the meanings that apply to your tests, classroom reading, and homework.

How to Use This Book

Most dictionaries just list all words in alphabetical order. That's a good idea, of course. But I have gone one step further. My WhizWords are in alphabetical order, but I have also divided them into six categories:

English-Language Arts	**Science**
History-Social Science	**Test Instructions**
Math	**All-Purpose Words**

This way, you can focus on the subjects where you want to improve your vocabulary. (Notice that I also included a list of words that you'll probably come across when you're taking tests, and another list of general words that you'll find useful in all your classes.)

Now, each of these chapters has two parts—the vocabulary list, plus some practice exercises. The exercises will help you remember important words that are related to each other. Off to the side of the exercises, you'll see a bunch of icons. These tell you what resources you'll use to do the exercise—things like TV, newspapers, and the Internet. These are the icons:

Life   School   Movie   Sports   Magazine

History   Fantasy   News   Internet   Television

These exercises are like dessert. The main course of the book is my WhizWord lists. The lists give you easy-to-understand definitions and sample sentences like the one I gave you for "impartial." You'll also find all this extra cool stuff:

   My helpful hints on how to learn words and ace tests.

   Really short quizzes to help cement the words in your brain.

   Good stuff to know that is related to a WhizWord.

DOUBLE MEANING   WhizWords that can mean two different things.

   Words that mean the same thing as a WhizWord.

   Words that mean the opposite of a WhizWord.

Related Word   An important word related to a WhizWord.

On the Test   How WhizWords are likely to appear on tests.

Okay then. I think I'm done explaining. Have fun, and remember, if you learn all these words, your vocabulary will be really, really good and you should do better on your tests. It's a groovy way to live. Peace.

Les Angeles

Chapter 1
English-Language Arts

Whiz Quiz

Use an adjective or adverb to describe each of these words:
chewy
green
school
shopping
sports
tests

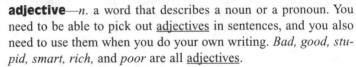

Related Word

analysis—n.
close study.

adjective—*n*. a word that describes a noun or a pronoun. You need to be able to pick out <u>adjectives</u> in sentences, and you also need to use them when you do your own writing. *Bad, good, stupid, smart, rich,* and *poor* are all <u>adjectives</u>.

adverb—*n*. a word that describes a verb, an adjective, or another adverb. What I just said for adjectives goes for <u>adverbs</u>. You can remember what words an <u>adverb</u> modifies because the parts of speech it modifies are part of its name: ad- (adjectives, adverbs) and -<u>verb</u> (verbs). *Very, really, not, incredibly, amazingly,* and *obviously* are all <u>adverbs</u>.

alliteration—*n*. the appearance of two or more words with the same initial sound in a sentence or phrase. *Example*: Slothy S. Slothster sank slowly into the sofa, sighing.

analogy—*n*. a comparison between two things made in order to explain an idea. *Example*: During the presidential election controversy in 2000, Bush and Gore supporters disagreed about practically everything. Oil and water definitely do not mix.

analyze—*v*. to study carefully to figure out something. I must say, after <u>analyzing</u> all the latest Internet search engines, I still like Yahoo! the best. It is fast, gets me the best results, and is easiest to navigate.

assonance—*n*. a partial rhyme where the vowels rhyme, but the consonants do not. *Example*: The wave should have stayed, but it left, which was best.

antonym—*n*. the opposite word. *Good* is the <u>antonym</u> of *bad*. *Over* is the <u>antonym</u> of *under*. I have listed <u>antonyms</u> for lots of words throughout this book.

bias—*n*. in English-Language Arts, it means point of view. Some tests will ask you to figure out the writer's <u>bias</u>. That means from which point of view is the writer writing. *Example*: Someone who writes a positive article about Corky Carroll can be said to have a pro-Corky Carroll <u>bias</u>.

cause and effect—*n*. an action and its result. The <u>cause and effect</u> in my screenplay involves a nasty feud between two actresses (cause), but I can't give the end (effect) away.

characteristics—*n*. special qualities. In English-Language

Arts, physical <u>characteristics</u> usually describe a character in a story or the story's setting. For example, some <u>characteristics</u> of Frankenstein include a high, square forehead and rivets coming out of the sides of his head.

chronological—*adj.* in the order events happened. Tests are always asking you to put events in <u>chronological</u> order, or to be able to take a set of <u>chronological</u> events and write a story about them. Jim Carrey's best movies, in <u>chronological</u> order, are *Ace Ventura: Pet Detective* (1994), *Ace Ventura: When Nature Calls* (1995), *Liar Liar* (1997), and *How the Grinch Stole Christmas* (2000).

clarify—*v.* to make clearer. On tests, you will often be asked to <u>clarify</u> sentences and what characters in stories are talking about. *Example*: "Jim Carrey's comedic brilliance over the span of his film career is unsurpassed in the history of cinema" can be <u>clarified</u> as "Jim Carrey is funnier than anyone, ever."

cliché—*n.* a saying that is used too much. It is a <u>cliché</u> to call cafeteria food dog food, because so many people have called it dog food before. In general, when writing a story, you want to avoid using <u>clichés</u>.

climax—*n.* the peak of a dramatic narrative. The <u>climax</u> of my favorite movie, *Jaws*, involves three men on a sinking boat, a large shark, and an exploding canister or two.

coherent—*adj.* making sense. It is important that sentences and paragraphs have a <u>coherent</u> structure. If you are telling a story, the first thing comes first, the second thing comes second, and so on. It is also important for people to be <u>coherent</u>. Newscasters, for instance, have to be <u>coherent</u> so we can understand what they're saying.

compare—*v.* to find the similarities in two or more things. (See the definition of *contrast*.)

compelling—*adj.* very interesting. The only way to keep readers interested in a story is to create *compelling* characters.

complex—*adj.* complicated, made up of a bunch of connected parts. On lots of tests you are asked to read <u>complex</u> passages and find the important information in them. It's like watching a murder mystery on TV and trying to figure out who did it. The mys-

WhizTip

To remember
characteristics,
think of the word
"character"—
characters have
characteristics.

Antonym

incoherent—adj.
confusing.

Antonym

simple—adj.
easy.

tery is <u>complex,</u> but if you pay attention and concentrate, you can figure out who the culprit is.

compound—*adj.* in English-Language Arts, a word made of two or more other words is a compound word. *Carpetbagger* (carpet + bagger) is a <u>compound</u> word. (See History-Social Science for the definition of *carpetbagger*.) <u>Compound</u> sentences are two sentences connected with a conjunction or a conjunction with a comma. *Example*: I really like her, but I am afraid to talk to her.

concise—*adj.* short and to the point. When you are writing, try to be <u>concise</u>. Judge Judy on TV is very concise in her rulings. She usually says something like "You're wrong, you're an idiot, you're guilty!" Now that's <u>concise</u>.

conflict—*n.* a clash of ideas; a clash of characters. Most interesting writing centers around <u>conflict</u>—two people who can't stand each other, or two ideas that are really different. For example, I am writing a screenplay called *Pretty Dumb* about two actresses who can't stand each other. There is a lot of <u>conflict</u> between the two.

consistent—*adj.* in agreement; compatible. On tests, your answers should be <u>consistent</u> with the information you are given.

contemporary—*adj.* of this time. In English-Language Arts, the word is usually used when talking about <u>contemporary</u> writers, which means writers who are writing stuff now. R. L. Stine is a contemporary writer. So is J. K. Rowling.

context—*n.* the setting a word or statement appears in. It's important to know <u>context</u> when you are trying to figure out what someone means. If someone yells "Stop!" the <u>context</u> of that yell tells you why he is yelling. Is his car being stolen? Or is he going to drive off a cliff? If you know the <u>context</u>, you will understand what he means.

contrast—*v.* to find the differences. This word is most often used in test questions that ask you to "compare and <u>contrast</u>." That just means write about the similarities AND the differences. *Example*: Compare and <u>contrast</u> supermodel/actress James King and actress/pin-up star Pamela Anderson.

credible—*adj.* believable. In a trial, a <u>credible</u> witness is a witness the jury can believe. On a test, a <u>credible</u> answer is one that you think could be true. So if I said Pamela Anderson and James King were both the best actresses in the world, that's not really a <u>credible</u> statement. If I said both are blonde and beautiful—that's <u>credible</u>.

denouement—*n.* the final outcome of the plot of a play, movie, or book. The <u>denouement</u> of my screenplay *Pretty Dumb* involves Pamela Anderson, James King, Fabio the producer, and a mystery third actress.

dialect—*n.* how a particular part of a country speaks. Where you come from is usually where you get your <u>dialect</u>. Authors

To remember credible means "believable," think of incredible, which means "really hard to believe."

use <u>dialect</u> in stories to give readers information about character and setting.

dialogue—*n.* the spoken conversations written in a book or a play, usually in quotation marks. Here's some <u>dialogue</u> from *Pretty Dumb*, the screenplay I'm writing for supermodel James King and actress Pamela Anderson. "Oh Pam—my blonde hair is a mess. Poor me. What brand of conditioner do you use?" asked James. "I use Fanteen Selectives, with blonde highlights," Pamela replied, "but you can't borrow it."

editorialize—*v.* to state one's opinion on a subject. Go to the <u>editorial</u> section of your local newspaper for examples of <u>editorializing</u>.

euphemism—*n.* an inoffensive term that is substituted for an offensive term. My dad uses the <u>euphemism</u> "You came up a little short" when he really means "You failed miserably." His <u>euphemism</u> makes failing miserably feel less discouraging!

evaluate—*v.* to consider. Tests ask you to <u>evaluate</u> information all of the time. That just means you need to read everything and consider the information before choosing an answer. My mom often <u>evaluates</u> the food she is buying at the grocery store by looking at the ingredients to see how much fat is in it. She hates fat.

expository—*adj.* related to giving meaning. An <u>expository</u> statement is a statement that explains the writer's position clearly and in detail. If you are asked to write an <u>expository</u> essay, your teacher wants you to explain or describe your subject in detail.

fallacy—*n.* a false notion; something that's not true. It is a <u>fallacy</u> to assume that just because the Dodgers haven't been to the World Series in years, they will never be there again. At least I hope it's a <u>fallacy</u> to assume that.

figurative language—*n.* the use of metaphors. Instead of writing "Tim Brown is a great football player," a sports reporter using <u>figurative language</u> would write "Tim Brown is a football player as great as the Rocky Mountains are tall." (See the definition for *metaphor* for more on this.)

flashback—*n.* a point in a story where the narrative goes back in time for a little while before continuing forward. Books and movies use <u>flashbacks</u> all the time, usually to give you more information about a character or the plot. Sometimes in movies and on TV, they signal a <u>flashback</u> by making the screen get all wiggly or fuzzy.

foreshadow—*v.* to hint at what is to come later in a story. A writer may <u>foreshadow</u> that two young characters are going to get married later in the book by having each of them, separately, talk to people about how much they want to get married when they get older.

List three
euphemisms
you or your
parents use:

1. _____
   _____
2. _____
   _____
3. _____
   _____

Remember
flashback by
thinking of the
word "back."

Remember
foreshadow by
thinking of the
word "forward."

genre—*n.* a type of writing. Romance, horror, mystery, and sci-fi are all fiction <u>genres</u>. My favorite <u>genre</u> is horror, especially R. L. Stine horror.

haiku—*n.* a three-line Japanese poem constructed with lines five, seven, and five syllables long. *Example*:

> *I met John Madden.*
>
> *He told me, Don't surf all day.*
>
> *Watch football instead.*

identify—*v.* to pick out. Tests often ask you to <u>identify</u> the protagonist or to <u>identify</u> the verb or to <u>identify</u> the simile.

idiom—*n.* word or phrase that means something it doesn't really mean. Confused? Here are a few <u>idioms</u>:

- *ants in your pants* means *you are fidgety*
- *born with a silver spoon in your mouth* means *your parents are rich*
- *stop bugging me* means *stop bothering me*

imagery—*n.* mental pictures; the use of figurative language to create scenes and moods. Writers use <u>imagery</u> to make their stories more interesting. Here's an example from my screenplay, with the <u>imagery</u> underlined: Pamela Anderson rose from bed and <u>stretched like a baby bird breaking from its egg</u>. She had a hard day ahead. She and James King were up for the same part in the new Jim Carrey movie. Whoever got the part would be the toast of the town. Whoever lost would feel <u>lower than the dirt on the soles of their six-inch stiletto heels</u>. The movie's producer, Fabio, would make his decision today.

interpret—*v.* to explain. It means you consider the information you have and try to figure out what it means. *Example*: In my screenplay, you can <u>interpret</u> a long silence between Pamela Anderson and James King to mean that each is busy thinking about how to beat the other one out for the prized part in the Jim Carrey movie. There are a lot of long silences.

irony—*n.* the use of words that mean the opposite of what you mean. A good example is when you say "Gee, I can't wait to go to the dentist and get those cavities filled" in a sarcastic tone, when going to the dentist is obviously the last thing you want to do.

juxtapose—*v.* to place side by side for comparison. By <u>juxtaposing</u> two very different characters in a story, their differences are further highlighted.

literal—*adj.* the real, dictionary meaning. What a word or phrase or any kind of writing or speaking actually means. "Go jump in a lake" usually doesn't mean someone wants you to get wet. But the <u>literal</u> meaning of the phrase is exactly that—go take a leap into the nearest pond, buddy.

metaphor—*n.* figurative use of words in which a word or phrase is used to mean something other than what it usually means. As you can probably tell by now, English-Language Arts is all about using words in creative ways, just like the fine arts are about using paint and clay in creative ways. For a creative writer, <u>metaphors</u> are as important as paint is for an artist. In my screenplay *Pretty Dumb*, I use <u>metaphors</u> all the time. Here are a couple: Fabio was a filmmaking *machine*, churning out two to three movies a year. Pamela's career was in *overdrive*. Every part she wanted, she got. (See the definition for *simile*—it's a lot *like* <u>metaphor</u>.)

modify—*v.* to change in part. I have been modifying my screenplay continuously since I finished the first draft. In fact, the current version bears little resemblance to that first draft, it has undergone so many <u>modifications</u>.

motivation—*n.* in English-Language Arts, it is the reason a character does something. Tests often ask you to write down a character's <u>motivation</u>. In my screenplay for *Pretty Dumb*, James King ended up talking about Pamela Anderson behind her back. What was James' <u>motivation</u>? You look for the part of the story that made James trash Pamela.

myth—*n.* a story about gods and heroes. My favorite <u>myth</u> is about the snake-haired Medusa: If you look right at her, you turn into Stone Phillips! Or do you just turn to stone? I can't remember.

narrative—*n.* a story. The <u>narrative</u> in *Pretty Dumb* follows two actresses as they angle for the starring role in a romantic comedy starring Jim Carrey.

objective—*adj.* unaffected by emotions or other outside forces. It is impossible for me to be <u>objective</u> about my screenplay because I am so close to it. But some <u>objective</u> readers, like my sister, have told me they like it.

omniscient—*adj.* all-knowing. You'll see this word used in the phrase "<u>omniscient</u> narrator," which describes a narrator in a story who "knows" everything that is going on and shares that information with the reader.

onomatopoeia—*n.* the use of words that imitate the sound they signify. *Buzz* and *splat* are good examples of <u>onomatopoeia</u>.

paraphrase—*v.* to express something using different words. Tests often ask you to <u>paraphrase</u> a statement or a character's views. That just means you write down what was said or what a character thinks in simple terms. I have to be able to <u>paraphrase</u> my screenplay *Pretty Dumb* in just a few words when I go try to sell it to Hollywood. Here it goes: Three days, two blonde actresses, one juicy movie role.

parody—*n.* a humorous mockery. <u>Parodies</u> mimic "normal" writing genres like horror, mystery, and romance. A good movie example of a <u>parody</u> is *The Pink Panther* series, starring Peter

Write the following sentences using metaphors:

Pam is fast.

James is tired.

Fabio likes ice cream a lot.

On the Test

What was Bill's motivation for continuing in the race?

You can remember paraphrase by thinking of the word "phrase." You are replacing a long piece of writing with a simple phrase.

Sellers, from the 1960s and '70s. It is a parody of "normal" detective movies. Watch it—you will laugh and laugh and laugh.

persuade—*v.* to convince. Writers will often try to <u>persuade</u> the readers that their point of view is correct. Tests often ask you to figure out what the writer is trying to <u>persuade</u> you to think. I am <u>persuading</u> you to learn the word <u>persuade</u>. <u>Persuaded</u>?

platitude—*n.* a statement that's a cliché. "The early bird gets the worm" is a <u>platitude</u>. "Slow and steady wins the race" is a <u>platitude</u>.

point of view—*n.* one way of looking at things. A character's <u>point of view</u> is that character's way of thinking. For example, in my screenplay *Pretty Dumb*, it is James King's <u>point of view</u> that Pamela Anderson is too old for the female lead in a Jim Carrey movie. Pamela Anderson's <u>point of view</u> is that James King is a silly supermodel who would turn the Jim Carrey movie into a disaster. Each tries to persuade the movie's producer, Fabio, that her <u>point of view</u> is the correct one.

premise—*n.* the basis for a story. The <u>premise</u> of my screenplay *Pretty Dumb* is two blonde actresses are gunning for the same part, and the person who decides who gets the part, Fabio, is evil.

preposition—*n.* a word that relates a noun or a pronoun to the other words in the sentence. Some popular prepositions are: *by, at, to, with, in, for, from*. What's that spell? BATWIFF. (You swing the bat, you whiff.) Cherish it. Remember it.

propaganda—*n.* the kind of writing that a government or group uses to get you to believe something. <u>Propaganda</u> is used all the time during wars, when one country tells its citizens that the other country is the worst country in the world. And the other country has <u>propaganda</u> that says the same thing about the first country. With <u>propaganda</u>, facts aren't important—it is convincing readers to believe something that is important.

prophecy—*n.* a prediction. <u>Prophecies</u> often have to do with the end of the world and stuff like that. In my screenplay *Pretty Dumb*, Pamela Anderson goes to a fortune teller, who makes a <u>prophecy</u> that Pamela will get a big part in a big movie starring a famous comedian.

relevant—*adj.* pertaining to the matter at hand. Tests often tell you to "consider the <u>relevant</u> information" before choosing your answer. You can remember what <u>relevant</u> means by thinking of the word *related*. <u>Relevant</u> information is *related* to the question.

resolution—*n.* the end of a story; how something is resolved. If there is a question about a story's <u>resolution</u>, that means the question is about how it ends. I don't want to give away the <u>resolution</u> of my screenplay *Pretty Dumb*, but let's just say there's some hair pulling and a few stiletto heels get broken . . . .

revise—*v.* to edit; to correct and improve. Sometimes you have

Write down your favorite (or least favorite) platitude:
_____
_____
_____

Write down the premise of the last movie you saw:
_____
_____
_____
_____
_____
_____

To remember prophecy, think of the word "prophet." In the Bible, prophets predict what God is going to do.

to <u>revise</u> a report for class. That means edit it and make it clearer. My mom asked me to <u>revise</u> my screenplay so her favorite singer, Barbra Streisand, could make a cameo appearance.

rhetorical—*adj.* fancy or artificial use of language. <u>Rhetorical</u> questions often don't have "real" answers. *Example*: What in heaven's name will I do if I don't ace this test?

similarities—*n.* common qualities; traits that are almost the same. Tests are always asking you about <u>similarities</u> and differences in characters, plots, settings, and stories. Being able to pick out <u>similarities</u> and differences means you understand what you are reading. (See the definitions for *compare* and *contrast* for more on this.)

simile—*n.* a comparison of unlike things that uses the words *like* or *as*. James is crazy <u>like</u> a fox. Pamela is smart <u>as</u> a whip. (By the way—those examples are both also *clichés*.)

speculate—*v.* to think about; to guess at. You are often asked to <u>speculate</u> as to why a character did what he did. That means you need to think about who that character is and why he would do what he did. For example, if you are asked to <u>speculate</u> as to why Fabio stops returning calls from both James King and Pamela Anderson, you would have to look at the actresses' behavior and why Fabio might get sick and tired of talking to them after a while.

stereotype—*n.* a judgment based on oversimple assumptions. You are using a <u>stereotype</u> when you think a person or group of people are a certain way for no real reason. *Example*: Italian Americans are often <u>stereotyped</u> as being in the Mafia. Blonde women are often <u>stereotyped</u> as being ditzy. Obviously, a <u>stereotype</u> has nothing to do with an individual person.

subordinate—*adj.* of lesser importance or rank. The word is often used to describe a <u>subordinate</u> clause, which depends on the main clause in a sentence. (I'll underline the <u>subordinate</u> clause in the following sentence.) <u>While James and Pamela grow to dislike each other more and more</u>, their agents fall in love. Aww!

summary—*n.* a short recap of the main points of a story. One of the main things you do in English-Language Arts class is <u>summarize</u> what you read. The best way to write a <u>summary</u> is to recap the story in the order things happened, so you don't forget anything.

suspense—*n.* the state of not knowing what will happen, otherwise known as the thing that puts you on the edge of your seat. Writers use <u>suspense</u> all of the time to keep you turning the pages. If you already know what's going to happen, why read on? In my screenplay, I use <u>suspense</u> the whole way—you don't find out which actress gets the part in the Jim Carrey movie until the very end.

symbolism—*n.* the use of an object to stand for something that

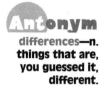

Antonym
differences—**n.**
things that are,
you guessed it,
different.

WhizQuiz

Write a
one-sentence
summary **of**
the last book
you read.

_____

_____

_____

_____

isn't there. *Example*: There are a lot of memorials in Washington, DC, that <u>symbolize</u> the soldiers who lost their lives in our wars. Writers use <u>symbolism</u> when they need to say something without really saying it. An example of this is when a writer <u>symbolizes</u> the passing of seasons by following a leaf as it falls from a tree and decays on the ground, and then feeds the roots of the tree it fell from.

synonym—*n.* a word that means the same thing as another word. *Daring* and *adventurous* are <u>synonyms</u>. *Timid* and *cowardly* are <u>synonyms</u>. When you are writing, instead of using the same word over and over, try to use <u>synonyms</u> to change things up a little bit. So if you use the word *car* in the first sentence, use *automobile* in the second and *vehicle* in the third.

thesis—*n.* a hypothetical argument. When you write a <u>thesis</u>, you are making a statement that you then have to back up with facts and arguments.

timeline—*n.* a graphical representation of a chronology; having a bunch of dates in chronological order on a line. <u>Timelines</u> are all over tests. Sometimes you have to write a story from a <u>timeline</u>. Sometimes you have to read a timeline to see what happened in what order. Here's an example from my screenplay:

Related Word

synonymous—adj. having the same meaning, but in a larger sense. Michael Jordan is synonymous with pro basketball. Hollywood is synonymous with the state of California.

 Pretty Dumb: Monday

9am—Pamela meets with Fabio	1pm—Pamela and James have lunch	3pm—Pamela goes on *Extra* and trashes James	7pm—James and Pamela get in a fight at the Golden Globes
10am—James meets with Fabio		5pm—James goes on *Access Hollywood* and trashes Pamela	11pm—Fabio has a late-night meeting with a mystery actress

Antonym

comedy—n. a funny play with a funny ending.

tragedy—*n.* in English-Language Arts, a tragedy is a serious play with a very sad ending. Shakespeare wrote the best <u>tragedies</u>, like *Hamlet* and *Macbeth*. My screenplay *Pretty Dumb* is kind of a <u>tragedy</u>: in the end, nobody wins. Neither James nor Pamela gets the part. Fabio gives it to Barbra Streisand instead. James quits the business and becomes a hermit in a windowless shack in Montana. Pamela pays the bills selling chicken roasters on the Home Shopping Network. But their agents get married and live happily ever after. Aww! The End.

Related Word

non-verbal communication, also known as body language, is the talking you do without speaking. For example, shrugging your shoulders means "I don't know."

verbal—*adj.* having to do with talking and words. The <u>verbal</u> sections of tests are about words, reading, and vocabulary.

verifiable—*adj.* provable; able to be checked. Something that is <u>verifiable</u> is something that can be proved with facts. Your age is <u>verifiable</u>—you just have to show your birth certificate.

WhizWords

analyze
clarify
compare
contrast
evaluate

English-Language Arts
Thinking Big

Lots of times when you're taking tests, you're asked to write down a date or name that you have memorized. These kinds of test questions basically test your memory. If you remember what you memorized, you'll be just fine.

But sometimes you have to do a little more than just remember. Sometimes you have to really think about information on the test, and figure out on your own what you think and how you should write it down. These kinds of questions ask you to **analyze** a problem; **evaluate** the situation; **compare** and con-**trast** ideas; and **clarify** your answer.

When these words appear in test questions, some kids freeze because they know a lot is expected of them—at least a lot more than just writing down a simple definition for a history test or identifying a shape on a geometry test. A good way to stop yourself from freezing is to get used to **analyzing, evaluating, comparing** and **contrasting,** and **clarifying** in situations that aren't so scary.

Whiz Tip

One great way to build your vocabulary is to hear the words read aloud. So, until they make an audio version of this book, ask an adult to play an audio book you like when you are driving around. Your local library probably has lots of audio books, just like mine. I personally like to listen to the *Harry Potter* books.

GETTING DEEP EXERCISE

In this exercise you are going to think deep about shallow things that you know a lot about. First, go back to the English-Language Arts WhizWords and refresh your memory about what these five words mean. Now pick a movie star, TV star, or entertainer you actually like or know a lot about. I am going to use Britney Spears as my victim, er, subject.

Write your subject at the top of the page. Now write down our five "getting deep" words along the left side of a piece of paper, about five lines apart. Next to each word, write down a topic relating to your victim, er, subject. Then write a short paragraph that answers the "questions" you have written. Here's mine:

Britney Spears

Analyze her album, *Oops . . . I Did It Again.*
Evaluate her singing.
Clarify her relationship with Justin Timberlake.
Compare and contrast Britney Spears and Christina Aguilera.

Once you have done this with one subject, pick another one and do it again. Keep practicing and you'll get really good at this. The more you see and use these words, the more comfortable you will get with them, and the better you'll do on your tests.

WhizWords

analogy
dialogue
figurative language
flashback
foreshadow
imagery
irony
metaphor
simile
symbolism

English-Language Arts
Writers' Tools

Good writers know how to use all sorts of tools to keep readers' eyes glued to the page (that's a **metaphor**, by the way). Some writers are so good at it, you just can't stop reading. I keep a flashlight under my bed for nights when my parents tell me to turn out my light and go to sleep, but I just can't stop reading. Good writers make writing look easy, so you don't notice all of the tools they are using.

But on tests, it's important to be able to pick out the tools writers use. Lots of reading questions on tests ask you to identify things like **metaphors, symbolism,** and **analogies**—basically all of the words that I have listed above on this page. The only way to learn how to find all of these things is to practice finding them in the stories you read every day.

IDENTIFYING A WRITER'S TOOLS EXERCISE

You are going to have to do a little hunting and gathering for this exercise. I want you to go through your house and get on the Internet and find examples of the following types of stories:

> Newspaper—sports story
> Magazine—fashion story
> Internet (print one out)—movie review
> Newspaper—article from the editorial page
> Internet (print one out)—piece of short fiction
> Magazine—celebrity profile
> Newspaper—political story

Gather these up in one place. Now, over the next week, I want you to read one of these stories every day and:

> 1. <u>Underline</u> the writers' tools.
> 2. Write the writer's tool in the margin.

There probably won't be enough room in the margins for some of these. If there isn't, you can write down the writer's tools you identify on Post-It Notes and stick them to the story.

WhizWords
Every adjective and adverb you can think of.

English-Language Arts
Adverbs and Adjectives

Imagine a world made up of only nouns and verbs. Actors would be . . . just actors. Not terrible actors, not handsome actors, not overpaid actors . . . just actors. Singers would be . . . just singers. Not gorgeous singers or over-produced singers or singers with voices that only a mother could love. Just . . . singers.

Luckily we have **adverbs** and **adjectives**, the words that make life special! Kevin Brown is the best pitcher in the league with a *sweet* curveball, *explosive* fastball, and *deceptive* change-up. The Dodgers are a *vastly improved* team with *incredible* talent and *limitless* potential.

Yes, **adjectives** and **adverbs**, the simple modifiers of verbs, nouns, and other **adjectives** and **adverbs,** give writing its spice. So it is very important to use them when you write. It makes your writing more interesting to read, which gets you better grades on your papers and writing tests. All good things, wouldn't you say?

WRITING YOUR AUTOBIOGRAPHY EXERCISE

If you don't believe me, let me prove it. I want you to try to describe your own life without adjectives and adverbs. Then I want you to describe your life WITH adjectives and adverbs—as many as you can possibly think of.

That's right—it's autobiography time. Grab a pencil and paper. Start by filling out this general outline. List three events in each age bracket that you will write about in your own journal or notebook. Stuff like losing your first tooth, learning to swim, moving to a new town, joining the basketball team—events that are memorable and important to you.

Age

0-4

5-8

9-present

Now write two versions of your autobiography: 1) using no adverbs or adjectives; and 2) using as many adverbs and adjectives as you can think of. Underline the adjectives and adverbs in the second version when you are done. I have provided you with a few adjectives and adverbs that you can use if you get stumped.

Adjectives and adverbs for your autobiography:
goofy
fast
unbelievable
slow
smelly
late
first
early
straight
green
gawky
crazy
funny
laughable
smart
right
heavenly
regrettable

Chapter 2
History-Social Science

Related Word
abolish—v. to get rid of.

abolitionist—*n.* someone who fought against slavery. When this country had slavery, there were a bunch of <u>abolitionists</u> trying to free the slaves. Some gave speeches, some ran the underground railroad—all of the <u>abolitionists</u> were working to stop a terrible system.

acculturation—*n.* the modification of one culture when it is exposed to another. When people from other countries immigrate to America, they go through a process of <u>acculturation</u> in which their "home" culture is influenced by American culture.

adapt—*v.* to change in response to the surroundings. The word is often used to describe how people and animals <u>adapt</u> as the environment changes. Charles Darwin found that animals <u>adapt</u> to their environments.

Name three rules at school that you advocate:

_____

_____

advocate—*n.* someone who supports a cause. My mom is a big <u>advocate</u> of the new dress code at school because she doesn't have to buy me expensive clothes anymore—just blue pants and a white shirt. If you <u>advocate</u> something, you support it.

aggressor—*n.* the person or country who attacks first. Germany was the <u>aggressor</u> in World War II.

industrial—adj. an economy based on industry (building things).

agrarian—*adj.* pertaining to a culture or economy based on farming and agriculture. The U.S. went from an <u>agrarian</u> economy in the 1800s to an industrial economy in the 1900s. Now there are hardly any farmers left.

allegiance—*n.* a deep commitment to something, like your country or your family. Of course, we have all pledged <u>allegiance</u> to the flag in school.

Related Word

ally—n. friend; someone in an alliance.

alliance—*n.* an association of people or nations coming together to achieve a common goal. Think of the TV show *Survivor*—the players try to form <u>alliances</u> to protect themselves from getting voted off the show.

ambition—*n.* a burning desire to achieve a goal or to become something. Madonna is often noted for her <u>ambition</u> to become famous. She doesn't have much singing talent, just tons of <u>ambition</u>. The same can be said of lots of actors and politicians.

WhizList

amendment—*n.* a change to the Constitution. We have had 27 amendments since the Constitution was adopted in 1789.

Related Word

amend—v. to correct or fix something.

amnesty—*n.* protection from prosecution; a pardon. Sometimes a government grants an individual amnesty. The largely black South African government granted their former white oppressors amnesty because they wanted the former white government officials to feel free to tell the truth about their terrible treatment of the country's black citizens.

anarchy—*n.* the state of having no government—or anyone else—in charge. Anarchy is usually thought of as a bad thing, with bands of hoodlums running around in the street, breaking windows, and beating people up. Sometimes after a team wins the World Series or the NBA Championship, there is anarchy in the streets when their fans go nuts and start turning over cars and lighting fires.

antebellum—*adj.* of the period prior to the Civil War. It's most often used in the phrase "the antebellum South," to describe the South before the Civil War. Think about the movie *Gone With the Wind*: southern gentlemen, women in hoop skirts, plantations—and slaves.

anthropology—*n.* the study of cultures. If you become an anthropologist, you will learn all about the thousands of different cultures that humans have formed.

archaeology—*n.* the study of remains from previous human life. If you become an archaeologist, you will be digging and diving for artifacts from previous generations.

artistocrat—*n.* a member of the nobility. Aristocrats used to rule the world. Born to their power, the aristocracy governed the "lower"classes in countries like England and France for centuries. Luckily, aristocracies never caught on here.

artifact—*n.* a tool or weapon from an ancient culture. I actually found an artifact myself when my family went camping in the Sierra Nevadas last year. I was digging for worms to use for fish bait when I found an arrowhead!

assimilate—*v.* to make similar or to absorb into a system or

History-Social Science

DOUBLE MEANING
assimilate—v.
to break food
down into its
nutrients and
absorb it (science).

culture. This word is often used when discussing how immigrants are absorbed into American culture. Assimilation is a complex process. Immigrants come here with their own customs. They want to keep some customs, but they also need to adopt some American customs. So the country assimilates them, but it is never easy.

barbarian—*n.* an uncivilized person, usually considered boorish and violent. Conan was a barbarian. What more can I say?

benevolent—*adj.* kind; caring. Most often used when talking about a "benevolent dictator," which means the dictator has total power, but he uses it for good, not evil. Superman would be a benevolent dictator.

WhizTip

One way to
remember
benevolent is to
imagine a nice
person named Ben:
like Ben Franklin
or Ben Affleck.

bias—*n.* prejudice. It usually means thinking someone is less than you are for a reason that doesn't make any sense, like gender or skin color. That is bias, or prejudice.

boom and bust economy—*n.* a kind of economy where things go incredibly well for a while, then crash and go incredibly poorly from there on out. It is most often used to describe the California gold rush in the 1800s, where everyone flocked to California for the boom, but once everyone was there and all of the gold had been mined, it all went bust.

boycott—*v.* to refuse to have dealings with a company or country because you disagree with something it does. It is a peaceful way to protest. Instead of picketing or doing something violent, people can boycott. Martin Luther King Jr. convinced black people to boycott the Montgomery, Alabama, bus system to protest segregation on the buses. That meant no black people would ride the buses, which meant the buses lost a lot of money. So then they had to pay attention to what Martin Luther King said, or they would go out of business.

buffalo soldiers—*n.* black soldiers who fought against the Native Americans during westward expansion. The Native Americans gave them the name buffalo soldiers because of the courage they displayed in battle.

bureaucracy—*n.* the non-elected officials in charge of the day-to-day business of the government. Bureaucracies are known for their inefficiency. Have you ever been with someone who is trying to get her driver's license renewed? And you were there half the day because the people who work there are slow and couldn't care less? That's bureaucracy in action!

DOUBLE MEANING
capital—n.
the city where
a state or nation's
government is
located.

capital—*n.* in economics, it means the wealth used to create more wealth. Basically, capital is money or property. If you were going to start a dot-com company, you would need some capital to start with—that includes money to pay your staff, a place to work, and some computers to work on.

capitalist—*n.* in economics, it is the person who owns the wealth used to create more wealth. Donald Trump is a famous capitalist.

carpetbagger—*n.* a politician who runs for office in a state she is not from. Most recently, Hillary Rodham Clinton was called a carpetbagger when she ran for elected office in New York, even though she was not from New York and had never lived there before, either.

caste—*n.* in India, one of four major hereditary classes of people. The important part: you are born into a caste. So if you are born into a "lower class" caste, that's where you will stay your whole life. You can't move up. Same with an "upper class" caste. You can't move down. Not like the United States at all.

censorship—*n.* restriction on what someone can say or do. Although the First Amendment to the Constitution protects our right to freedom of speech, television shows are censored, movies are censored, and songs are censored. Censorship happens every day in this country—usually to protect young people from adult language and situations. Many artists and performers are frustrated by censorship in the United States. Some countries, however, censor everyone on what he can say anywhere, anytime. This type of censorship is used to control people and prevent them from complaining about the government.

centralized—*adj.* focused in one person or area. In Social Studies, the word is usually used to talk about power and governments. A centralized government gives a lot of power to one person or group of people—like a king or a single ruling party. A *decentralized* government spreads that power out to a lot of people or groups of people.

checks and balances—*n.* when talking about the U.S. government, it is the system of government branches that each limit one another's power. So the president can do some things, but Congress has a say in what he does. Same with Congress—it can do some things, but the president also has a say. The judiciary branch—the courts—have a say in everything, too, and Congress and the president have a say in who gets to be a judge.

circumstances—*n.* the conditions and facts surrounding an event. In a recent surfing competition, circumstances worked against me. Everyone else kept getting great waves to ride, but I kept getting duds. Oh well—sometimes you can't control your circumstances.

civic—*adj.* relating to your city or town. This word is sometimes used when discussing your role as a citizen. People often say "It's your civic duty to vote." That just means that as a member of a community, you should take part in what is going on there.

civil disobedience—*n.* a kind of protest where someone refuses to obey civil laws because he doesn't believe in them. Civil

History-Social Science

disobedience is almost always nonviolent. Martin Luther King organized sit-ins to protest "whites-only" restaurants. Black people would simply sit at a table and not leave until the cops came and took them away.

coerce—*v.* to force someone to do something by threatening her. I was coerced into babysitting for my sister last weekend. My dad said if I didn't, I wouldn't get the new PlayStation—ever! You may have heard of the Coercive Acts that England forced on the American colonies (called the Intolerable Acts by the colonists) after the Boston Tea Party.

colonize—*v.* to establish a culture in a foreign land by putting some citizens there. It often results in those citizens taking over that foreign land. Not a very nice thing to do, but it has been a common practice for many countries, including the United States.

commerce—*n.* the act of buying and selling things. When you go to Wal-Mart and buy a notebook, you are engaging in commerce, and so is Wal-Mart.

commodity—*n.* something that is bought or sold. Like a notebook or a car or a ton of grain. They are all commodities.

communism—*n.* a system where the people own the factories, farms, and other property. At least that is the communist ideal. In most communist countries so far—like Cuba and the old Soviet Union—the government "owns" the property and most of the people have little say in how everything is run.

compassion—*n.* mercy. When I came in tenth out of ten at the surfing nationals, my dad showed compassion by not pointing out the things I did wrong, which was just about everything.

compensation—*n.* the amount paid for goods (stuff) or services (labor). When you get paid for doing something, you are getting compensation. When you pay for something, you are giving compensation.

compromise—*n.* a settlement where each side gives up something. So if you want to watch TV after dinner but your dad wants you to wash the dishes, a compromise would be watching TV, and then washing the dishes afterward.

conscription—*n.* the policy of forcing citizens to fight in wars. It's also called the draft. At different points in history, America has conscripted people into the armed forces, usually when there was a war on. At other times, the armed forces have been made up of volunteers.

consensus—*n.* collective opinion; general agreement. The general consensus at the surfing nationals was that Biff Hardaway would win.

consent—*n.* permission. In History-Social Science, it is often used to describe elected officials serving at the "consent of the governed." That means we put them into office by voting for them, and we can get rid of them if we want.

consequences—*n.* the results of something that happened. As a parent or teacher must have told you at some point in your life, there are <u>consequences</u> for your actions. In Social Studies, the word is usually used when talking about something bad that happened, like Japan bombing Pearl Harbor (<u>consequence</u>: the U.S. joined the war) or the Watergate scandal (<u>consequence</u>: Nixon resigned). But <u>consequences</u> can also stem from positive events.

constitution—*n.* the laws that govern a group of people, usually a country or a state. The U.S. <u>Constitution</u> has in it the basic laws that we follow in this country.

controversy—*n.* a situation where two sides have opposing views, and people have a hard time figuring out who is right. There was a huge <u>controversy</u> at my school last year when my friend Ralph refused to wear the new uniform—and his parents agreed with him! The principal called an assembly, Ralph's parents were in and out of school almost every day, Ralph was suspended, and it was in the newspaper!

covenant—*n.* a binding agreement; a compact. It's basically promising something, cross-your-heart, hope to die, stick a needle in your eye. A serious promise.

crusade—*n.* a serious movement for a cause. I have been <u>crusading</u> for a middle-school surf team at school for the past year. We have tennis, golf, basketball, and soccer. Why not surfing?

currency—*n.* a country's money. Our <u>currency</u> is dollars, the British use pounds, and the Japanese use yen.

democracy—*n.* a government where the people hold the power. We have a representative <u>democracy</u>, which means we elect representatives to do what we, the people, want them to do.

deprive—*v.* to take away. In History-Social Science, the word is often used to talk about people being <u>deprived</u> of their rights. That means they don't have any rights to do what they want to do. When my friend Ralph's parents were against the dress code, they said Ralph was being <u>deprived</u> of his right to dress how he wants.

despotism—*n.* rule by a despot, someone who has absolute power and can do whatever he wants. Hitler was a <u>despot</u> in Germany. Saddam Hussein is a <u>despot</u> in Iraq. There are still lots of <u>despots</u> around the world.

diplomat—*n.* a person who represents her country while living in another country. Most countries have <u>diplomats</u> in other countries, so if something happens, say, in Mexico, the United States' <u>diplomat</u> in Mexico can make sure the United States' interests are kept in mind.

discriminate—*v.* to treat someone badly for unfair reasons.

On the Test
What were three
consequences of
the American
Revolution?

WhizFact
The Mayflower
Compact was
a covenant signed
by the 41 male
passengers on the
Mayflower, saying
they would
stick together.

WhizTip
To remember
despotism, think
of the word
"despicable."

Related Word
diplomatic—adj.
good at dealing
with people and
their problems.

History-Social Science

Black people have been <u>discriminated</u> against a lot in our country. Even my second favorite sport, baseball, <u>discriminated</u> against black people until 1947, when Jackie Robinson became the first black man in the Major Leagues. And racial <u>discrimination</u> still exists—there may be tons of black players, but there are hardly any black managers.

dissent—*n.* disagreement. In America, you have the right to register your <u>dissent</u>, no matter what you think. It's called freedom of speech. My friend Ralph's parents had every right to register their <u>dissent</u> with the school's dress code. They lost—Ralph had to wear the uniform like the rest of us, but they still had the right to disagree.

diversity—*n.* variety. In History-Social Science, the word is usually used to talk about the <u>diversity</u> of opinions (lots of different opinions) and the <u>diversity</u> of cultures (lots of different cultures) that make up America. Some call our <u>diversity</u> a melting pot, some call it a quilt—the point is, we have a very <u>diverse</u> society.

doctrine—*n.* a set of beliefs that defines a group. The word is most often used to talk about a country's or church's <u>doctrine</u>— its set of written rules. I saw the pope on TV the other day and he was talking about Christian <u>doctrine</u> of "love thy neighbor as thyself."

dogmatic—*adj.* arrogantly assertive, with no facts to back up the assertions. I can be <u>dogmatic</u> when I talk about surfing legend Corky Carroll. I think he's the coolest dude who ever walked the face of the Earth, but he's never held down a steady job.

domestic—*adj.* having to do with home. You may have heard the phrase "<u>domestic</u> affairs"—that refers to issues within a country, not in other countries.

dominate—*v.* to take precedence; to be most important. Combining the definition above with this one, you may have heard of "domestic affairs <u>dominating</u> Congress" or something along those lines. That means issues close to home are taking up most of the time and effort in Congress. Different issues tend to <u>dominate</u> in our culture, depending on all sorts of things: war and peace, the economy, the rights of people being respected or abused. All of these issues have <u>dominated</u> at one time or another.

due process—*n.* the established way our court system works. The phrase "You have a right to <u>due process</u>" is very important for this country. It means no matter who you are, you get treated the same—and fairly—in our court system.

economy—*n.* the combination of goods, services, and people and how they all work together to survive. We have a market <u>economy</u>, which means the laws of supply and demand determine who makes and gets what. The other kind of <u>economy</u> is a command <u>economy</u>, in which a government determines (commands) who makes and gets what. China has a command <u>economy</u>.

egalitarian—*adj.* having to do with equal rights for all. My school is not <u>egalitarian</u> when it comes to sports. They think basketball and soccer are the most important sports, and that surfing isn't even close to being their equal.

eligible—*adj.* qualified; available. An <u>eligible</u> voter is someone who is qualified to vote—this person is a citizen, has registered, is old enough, etc. An <u>eligible</u> bachelor is someone who is not married or dating anyone and would make somebody a good husband. I am an <u>eligible</u> bachelor.

emancipation—*n.* the act of gaining freedom. Our <u>emancipation</u> from England and the <u>emancipation</u> of slaves in our country are two pivotal moments in our history.

embargo—*n.* the prohibition of goods from entering or leaving a country. After the Gulf War, the United States put an oil <u>embargo</u> on Iraq so they couldn't sell oil to anyone anymore.

emigrate—*v.* to leave one's home country for another. This country is made up of millions of people who have <u>emigrated</u> from distant lands to find opportunity here. Orlando Hernandez is a major league pitcher who <u>emigrated</u> from Cuba.

enlighten—*v.* to inform. My sister <u>enlightened</u> me about why I would never get her room: she is bigger, stronger, and older, and couldn't care less how small my room is.

entrepreneur—*n.* someone who takes business risks in a capitalist economy. It can be someone who bets that if she is right about a business venture, she will get rich. <u>Entrepreneurs</u> start most of the new companies in our country every year, betting the business will succeed. Steve Jobs was an <u>entrepreneur</u> when he started Apple Computer in his garage in the 1970s. Martha Stewart took an ability to make pretty doilies and turned it into a multimillion dollar empire!

ethics—*n.* moral rules that govern individuals or groups. For example, medical <u>ethics</u> start with the promise that doctors "First, do no harm." That means a doctor must not make a patient any sicker than he already is.

expansion—*n.* growth. As in territorial <u>expansion</u>, it means a city or country keeps annexing the land that is next to it, and then the land next to that. The U.S. <u>expanded</u> from thirteen states on the East Coast all the way west to California, and then picked up Alaska and Hawaii, too. Now that's what I call <u>expansion</u>.

fascism—*n.* a government with a ruthless dictator, centralized control, and nationalist tendencies. Hitler was a <u>fascist</u>. So was Mussolini. The Allied Powers fought <u>fascism</u> in World War II and won. It's all my great-grandfather talks about.

federalism—*n.* a government with separate states that are unit-

---

Whiz Tip

The U.S. is called "the land of the free," so **emancipation** (freedom) is probably our most important ideal. That means you are lucky—but it also means lots of test questions on the subject.

On the Test

In what way was Christopher Columbus an **entrepreneur**?

ed under one larger government. The United States (get it—*united* states) is a <u>federalist</u> system. Alexander Hamilton was a big early advocate of <u>federalism</u>.

feminism—*n.* a movement committed to getting women the same rights and opportunities as men. Women make less money than men for the same work, and our society treats them differently in many ways. <u>Feminists</u> are out to change that so everyone is equal.

feudalism—*n.* an economic system in Europe that lasted throughout the Middle Ages, in which subjects and serfs had to serve their lords.

forfeit—*v.* to give up; to hand over. When one commits a crime and goes to jail, he <u>forfeits</u> a lot of his rights as a citizen, like the freedom to walk around and go wherever he wants. If your baseball team doesn't show up for a game, it <u>forfeits</u> the game, and loses automatically.

free enterprise—*n.* an economic system in which businesses can try to make a profit without the government getting in their way with lots of regulations. The United States has a <u>free enterprise system</u>.

frontier—*n.* an area of land where people don't live yet; the great unknown. The United States was once just a few states on the East Coast with a great <u>frontier</u> to its west that still "belonged" to the Native Americans. If you're a *Star Trek* fan, you've heard William Shatner say these words a million times: "Space—the final <u>frontier</u> . . . . These are the voyages of the Starship Enterprise. Its five-year mission: to explore strange new worlds, to seek out new life and new civilizations, to boldly go where no man has gone before." That's exactly how the pioneers felt when they packed up their covered wagons and headed out West.

fundamental—*adj.* basic. In this country we have certain <u>fundamental</u> rights—the rights to life, liberty, and the pursuit of happiness. Maybe you've heard of these somewhere?

futile—*adj.* useless. Lots of times people will tell you not to try, that trying is <u>futile</u>. Until the Dodgers got Kevin Brown, I thought the team's attempts to get to the World Series were futile. Now, I think it's just a matter of time.

grievances—*n.* complaints. The colonists had a list of grievances against mother England, the biggest of which was they were getting taxed a lot. I have a list of <u>grievances</u> I gave to my mother last week, the biggest of which was my allowance needs to be higher. The colonists rebelled. I hope my mom gets the hint!

hazardous—*adj.* dangerous. You've probably seen this word in ads for cigarettes: "CAUTION: Cigarette smoking may be <u>hazardous</u> to your health." Being an early colonist was also

Whiz Fact

Gloria Steinem and Betty Friedan are famous modern feminists. Elizabeth Cady Stanton is a famous suffragette—a woman who fought for women's right to vote in the early 20th century (see definition for suffrage).

Whiz Quiz

List three things you once thought were futile:

1. _____
2. _____
3. _____

definitely <u>hazardous</u> to one's health.

heretic—*n.* someone who speaks contrary to what a church teaches. In the Middle Ages, <u>heretics</u> had to watch out. Lots of times, <u>heresy</u> was punishable by death!

humanitarian—*adj.* helpful to humans. You've probably heard of the U.S. sending <u>humanitarian</u> aid to countries that need help. That basically means we send food and medicine. A couple years ago my school had a can and clothing drive and sent <u>humanitarian</u> aid to earthquake victims.

hunter–gatherer—*n.* someone who hunts animals and gathers other foods (vegetables, grains) as a way of life. In the 1700s, many Native Americans were <u>hunter–gatherers</u>.

immigration—*n.* the act of coming from a foreign country to live in a new country. America has grown in population over the years mainly due to <u>immigration</u>. The country practically begged people to <u>immigrate</u> here so it could push west over the frontier and fill up all of its land with new citizens.

impartial—*adj.* fair. Judges and juries are supposed to be impartial. That means they just go by the facts. Like Judge Judy on TV—she is an <u>impartial</u> judge who listens to all the facts, then she reams the person who is guilty.

impeachment—*n.* charging an elected official with doing something wrong. President Clinton was <u>impeached</u> a few years ago. It was only the second time in the history of the country a president was <u>impeached</u>. Clinton's <u>impeachment</u> hearings dominated the news for weeks.

imperialism—*n.* rule by an empire. A few hundred years ago, <u>imperialism</u> was the way to go. There was the Roman Empire, the Spanish Empire, the German Empire. These <u>imperial</u> governments would go out and conquer a bunch of countries so they could expand their empires. Of course America was part of the British Empire—<u>imperial</u> Britain—at one point.

impose—*v.* to force. My Spanish teacher <u>imposed</u> a "no English" rule last week in class, so no one could speak English in her class the whole week! If you did, you had to put your head on your desk for five minutes. It was really funny watching everyone mess up and put their heads on their desks.

inalienable—*adj.* unable to be taken away; unable to be separated from. Most often linked to Americans' <u>inalienable</u> rights of life, liberty, and the pursuit of happiness. One way to remember this word is to think about the word "alien." Space aliens are beings from other planets. So something that is *in*alienable is something that is *not* something from another planet.

inaugurate—*v.* to have a ceremony where a politician gets installed in office. George W. Bush was <u>inaugurated</u> in 2001 after a bitter election battle against Al Gore.

DOUBLE MEANING
humanitarian—n.
someone who is known for his work helping mankind. Jonas Salk was a great humanitarian—he discovered the vaccine for polio.

Whiz Quiz

Who was the first president to be impeached? Hint: It wasn't Bill Clinton.

DOUBLE MEANING
impose—v. to butt in. You may have heard people say "I don't mean to impose, but . . ." and then they go ahead and impose.

29

indigenous—*adj.* native. The people who are originally from a country are called the country's <u>indigenous</u> people. Native Americans are <u>indigenous</u> to North America—everyone else who lives in this country came here from somewhere else or is descended from someone who did.

inevitable—*adj.* going to happen; unavoidable. It is <u>inevitable</u> that you are going to have to take tests, so you might as well just get used to them. When something is unavoidable, my grandfather always says "It's as <u>inevitable</u> as death and taxes." I have my own expression "It's as <u>inevitable</u> as the next good wave, dude."

influence—*n.* the power to change something. The United States has incredible <u>influence</u> around the world. In 1936, a man named Dale Carnegie wrote a book called *How to Win Friends and Influence People*, and it became one of the best-selling books of all time because, well, that's what everyone wants, right?

inhabitants—*n.* people who live somewhere. You are an <u>inhabitant</u> of California. Prince Charles is an <u>inhabitant</u> of England.

innovation—*n.* a brand new way of doing something or a new device that is better than the previous device. The electric guitar was an <u>innovation</u> that allowed bands to play louder. Before the electric guitar, the only way to play loud was on an acoustic guitar aimed at a microphone.

instability—*n.* the state of being unsteady and insecure. When things are up in the air, when they can go one way or the other—that is <u>instability</u>. *Example*: There is <u>instability</u> on a baseball team when the players don't like the manager, and the manager doesn't like the players. Who is right—the players who say the manager is stupid or the manager who says the players are terrible? Who do you side with? All these questions lead to <u>instability</u>. It's the same with a country when there is <u>instability</u>. Usually, there is <u>instability</u> when there is a change in leaders. Maybe the army liked the old leader better, so they won't listen to the new leader. That leads to <u>instability</u>.

institution—*n.* a really well-known or well-established organization or person. There are real <u>institutions</u> like colleges (<u>institutions</u> for higher learning) and hospitals (health <u>institutions</u>). There are also people who are known as <u>institutions</u>—like Bill Cosby is a comedy <u>institution</u>, and Michael Jordan is a basketball <u>institution</u>. They are just *so important* to their fields, they are <u>institutions</u>.

insurgent—*n.* a person who revolts against authority. When you watch newscasters, you may hear them talk about "rebel <u>insurgents</u>" in other countries, and then show some guys with machine guns running around in the woods fighting against government forces.

insurrection—*n.* revolt against the people in charge. The word is used in the Declaration of Independence to describe the king of England's treatment of the colonies: "He has excited domestic <u>insurrections</u> amongst us." That means the colonists thought the king was turning them against each other.

integration—*n.* the creation of one group by combining different groups; having people of all different races living together instead of apart. Our country was segregated—white people and black people were separated from each other until the 1950s and 1960s, when segregation was made illegal. Now we are an <u>integrated</u> society—people of all races are allowed to live side by side.

interdependent—*adj.* depending on each other. Countries are getting more and more <u>interdependent</u>. Lots of countries rely on us for corn; we rely on lots of countries for oil; and everyone relies on France for French fries.

WhizTip

Think of the word "depend" to remember interdependent.

intervene—*v.* to butt in. I had to <u>intervene</u> on the playground last week when my friend Ralph and that jerk Frankie got into a fight. I was able to keep them apart until the teacher came.

intolerant—*adj.* unable to accept views one doesn't agree with. There are lots of <u>intolerant</u> people in the world—people who don't like other people just because they are different. Don't be <u>intolerant</u>. It will just make you mean.

invasion—*n.* an attack on another country and the taking over of their land. The D-Day <u>invasion</u> of Normandy in World War II in 1944 is the largest, and one of the most famous, <u>invasions</u> ever. The Allied forces caught the Germans by surprise and ended up driving them out of France.

isolate—*v.* to separate from everything else. When I was in kindergarten, I was a big spaz. Sometimes I got so hyper my teacher had to <u>isolate</u> me at nap time—she put up big dividers so I couldn't see the rest of the kids and they couldn't see me.

jeopardy—*n.* peril; danger. Think of the game show *Jeopardy*. If you go on that show, you are in <u>jeopardy</u> of looking really stupid if you can't answer any questions.

jurisdiction—*n.* an area of authority. The word <u>jurisdiction</u> is often used to talk about the courts having <u>jurisdiction</u> over a case. That means the case happened in a court's physical area. So if someone robbed someone in Orange County, the case would be tried in the <u>jurisdiction</u> of Orange County.

WhizTip

To remember jurisdiction, think of the word "jury." A case's jurisdiction is wherever a jury would be seated to try the case.

justify—*v.* give reasons for. I <u>justified</u> skipping class to surf by reasoning that if I didn't skip class, I would never be a pro surfer. My parents and teachers did not agree with my <u>justifications</u>. I was grounded *and* I got detention. Ouch.

laissez-faire—*adj.* favoring an economic doctrine that opposes government regulations. <u>Laissez-faire</u> economists think mar-

History-Social Science

kets solve problems best, not governments.

● **lame duck**—*n.* a politician who has some time left in her term, but her replacement has already been elected. So she is still doing her job, but she has already been voted out. That means she has little power left, and she's basically just keeping the seat warm for her successor.

● **legislation**—*n.* proposed laws. In the U.S. government, Congress writes and votes on <u>legislation</u>.

● **mandate**—*n.* the right to do something. In elections, when voters pick someone overwhelmingly, that politician has a <u>mandate</u>. That means the voters have told him—with their votes—that he can do what he wants because they agree with his plan. When a politician wins in a landslide (see the Related Word) he has a <u>mandate</u> from the voters. When there is a close election (like when George W. Bush barely beat Al Gore in 2000), there is not a <u>mandate</u> because lots of people voted for the guy who lost.

● **manifest destiny**—*n.* a policy of imperialist expansion that says a country can take over another country because God says so. Imperialist countries like England took over other countries using this concept of <u>manifest destiny</u>. The United States took over lots of its western lands by using this concept of <u>manifest destiny</u>. <u>Manifest destiny</u> is bad. It's basically just an excuse to take over a country.

● **maritime**—*adj.* having to do with shipping and navigation. Before planes and trains, <u>maritime</u> adventures were the only way to go for people who wanted to see the world.

● **mercenary**—*n.* a professional soldier. Mercenaries fight for whomever pays them to fight. There's even a magazine for <u>mercenaries</u> called *Soldier of Fortune*. Get it? They *soldier* so they can make a *fortune*.

● **metallurgy**—*n.* the science of extracting metals from their ores.

● **microcosm**—*n.* a detail of something bigger; a miniature version of something big. New York City is often called a <u>microcosm</u> of the world because there are immigrants from just about every country living there, speaking just about every language known to man.

● **migration**—*n.* the movement from one place to another. In the past 20 years, there has been a <u>migration</u> of people in this country from cold places like New York to warm places like Southern California.

● **militant**—*adj.* combative; warring. Some countries have <u>militant</u> histories, ours included.

● **misconception**—*n.* an incorrect assumption. My sister is under the <u>misconception</u> that I have given up trying to trade my tiny bedroom for her big bedroom. I have many more tricks up my sleeve.

Whiz Quiz

Go to
www.house.gov
and find a piece
of legislation
Congress is
working on now.

Related Word

landslide—n.
winning an
election by a
huge margin.

On the Test

Which was
the period of
greatest Mexican
migration?

32

mitigate—*v.* to moderate; to make less severe. When I skipped class to go surfing, I tried to <u>mitigate</u> the trouble I was in by explaining that on the way to the beach, I helped a little old lady cross the street. It didn't work.

moderate—*adj.* not extreme. <u>Moderate</u> temperatures are not too hot and not too cold. <u>Moderate</u> politicians are not too liberal and not too conservative.

monotheistic—*adj.* believing in one god. Christianity is a <u>monotheistic</u> religion. There are also polytheistic religions, like Hinduism, that worship many gods.

municipal—*adj.* related to a city or a town. You probably have heard of a <u>municipal</u> government and a <u>municipal</u> school system and <u>municipal</u> courts. That just means those things are located in a city—whatever city that may be.

mutual—*adj.* shared in common between two people, things, or groups. When something is done for the <u>mutual</u> benefit, that means both benefit. When Justin Timberlake and Britney Spears are seen in public together, they <u>mutually</u> benefit. All of her fans start to like him, and all of his fans start to like her.

mystic—*adj.* having to do with religious mysteries or occult practices. The fortune teller at the county fair claimed her crystal ball had <u>mystical</u> powers, but I kind of doubt it was true.

nationalism—*n.* loyalty to one's country. <u>Nationalism</u> is a good thing when it means you really like your country and are proud of it. <u>Nationalism</u> is a bad thing when it means you really like your country but hate all the other countries. Most often these days, when you hear about <u>nationalism</u>, it's when one country is beating up on another one out of a feeling of <u>nationalism</u>.

negotiate—*v.* to discuss something with the goal of reaching an agreement. Throughout history there have basically been two ways to solve disagreements—to fight or to <u>negotiate</u>. <u>Negotiating</u> is better, because nobody gets hurt.

nemesis—*n.* sworn enemy. The Joker is Batman's <u>nemesis</u>. Lex Luthor is Superman's <u>nemesis</u>. Christina Aguilera is Britney Spears' nemesis. The Soviet Union used to be the United States' <u>nemesis</u>.

neutral—*adj.* not taking sides. Lots of times, when two countries go to war, other countries remain <u>neutral</u>. That means they aren't taking sides in the war—they are staying out of it. The United States was <u>neutral</u> in World War II until Japan bombed Pearl Harbor.

nomad—*n.* a person with no fixed home who moves from place to place. My dad was a bit of a <u>nomad</u> before he married my mom. I think he lived in six different cities and three different countries before settling down.

History-Social Science

nullify—*v.* to void; to take something back. Sometimes, after an agreement has been negotiated, something happens and the agreement gets <u>nullified</u>. That means all the negotiating was wasted, because the agreement that was reached doesn't count. It happens all the time in baseball when a team is trying to make a trade, but the trade gets <u>nullified</u> when one of the players doesn't pass his physical.

obstacle—*n.* something that gets in the way. You have probably been in a race through an <u>obstacle</u> course where you have to run around some cones and climb a wall or two. My main <u>obstacle</u> at school is that I have a hard time paying attention, but I'm working on it.

oligarchy—*n.* government of and by a few people. <u>Oligarchy</u> is kind of the next step up from monarchy (rule by one person) but it's not even near democracy (rule by all of the people).

opportunity—*n.* chance. The United States has been called "the land of <u>opportunity</u>." And my dad is always saying "When <u>opportunity</u> knocks—open the door!" He loves that one.

opposition—*n.* someone who is against someone else. It looks like the Dodgers' main <u>opposition</u> this year as they try to get to the World Series is going to be the Atlanta Braves.

Name your favorite team's main opposition:

_____

oppress—*v.* to keep somebody down. This country has a history of <u>oppressing</u> black people and women. Thankfully, that <u>oppression</u> isn't nearly as bad now as it used to be.

orator—*n.* someone who gives speeches. It is important for a politician to be a good <u>orator</u>, because he has to give speeches that convince people to vote for him. President Bush is not a good <u>orator</u>—he can barely string together two sentences.

WhizTip

To remember orator think of "oral"—having to do with the mouth (speaking).

orthodox—*adj.* adhering to tradition, usually used when talking about religions. <u>Orthodox</u> religions usually take their texts (like the Bible, Torah, and Koran) literally, and have more rigid rules than reformed, or "modernized," versions of the same ancient religions.

paleolithic—*adj.* pertaining to the Stone Age, beginning almost 2 million years ago and ending about 15,000 years ago. The <u>paleolithic</u> era is marked by the use of stone tools.

partisan—*n.* a supporter of a political party; a supporter of a cause. You have probably heard of "<u>partisan</u> politics" in Washington, DC. That means our two major political parties—the Democrats and Republicans—are more interested in getting their way then getting something done. Being a <u>partisan</u>—a supporter of their party—is more important than doing what they were elected to do.

persecute—*v.* to oppress. The Nazis persecuted Jews in World War II. The Romans <u>persecuted</u> Christians for hundreds of years. European colonists <u>persecuted</u> Native Americans for hundreds of years. Unfortunately, the history of mankind is filled with <u>persecution</u>.

petition—*n.* a formal request to a government or another authority. You have probably signed a <u>petition</u> at some point in your life. Last year I signed a <u>petition</u> to end the dress code at my school, but it didn't work—we still have a dress code!

pivotal—*adj.* the most important. The <u>pivotal</u> moment of my school's last baseball game was when the other team had the bases loaded and our pitcher struck out their best hitter. That's what I call <u>pivotal</u>.

polarize—*v.* to cause two groups to focus on their differences. The issue of slavery <u>polarized</u> the United States in the 1800s. Half the states were for it, half were against it.

polis—*n.* a Greek city-state. A <u>polis</u> was a group of citizens who shared a government, religion, army, and economy. Athens and Sparta are both examples of a <u>polis</u>.

populism—*n.* a political philosophy that puts the needs of the "common people" first. <u>Populist</u> politicians usually talk about having the rich pay their fair share in taxes and redistributing the nation's wealth to the poorer people.

pragmatist—*n.* someone who is practical. A <u>pragmatist</u> tends to support things he thinks can actually be done. For example, a <u>pragmatist</u> would be satisfied if a last-place team just improved a little, and maybe the next year made it to the middle of the pack. He wouldn't expect the team to go from last place to first place in one year because that wouldn't be practical.

prejudice—*n.* an opinion reached about a person or event without knowing the facts. You can break the word down into its components: *pre* and *judge*. <u>Prejudice</u> is *prejudging* a person or situation. It is most often used when discussing racial <u>prejudice</u>.

preservation—*n.* protection from destruction. This word is used most often when people are talking about <u>preserving</u> old buildings in their town (historic <u>preservation</u>), and when people are talking about <u>preserving</u> the environment (environmental <u>preservation</u>).

principles—*n.* ideals; beliefs. A person who has <u>principles</u> is a person who does what he thinks is right, no matter what the consequences. Martin Luther King Jr. had <u>principles</u>. So did Che Guevara.

productive—*adj.* able to produce a lot of stuff. A <u>productive</u> writer writes a lot of books and articles. A <u>productive</u> farmer harvests a lot of crops. A <u>productive</u> hitter hits a lot of extra-base hits and gets a lot of RBIs.

profit—*n.* in business, the money left over after you subtract the costs of making something that you sell. If it costs a company $20 to make a CD player and they sell it for $50, their <u>profit</u> is $30.

WhizTip
To remember pivotal, think about "pivot," which means "to turn."

Antonym
idealist—n. someone who wants the best things possible to happen, no matter how impractical those things may be.

Related Word
self-preservation—n. the act of doing things that help you survive.

WhizFact
Shakespeare was a very productive writer, writing around 40 plays and hundreds of poems in his lifetime.

Related Word
profitable—adj. able to make a profit.

History-Social Science

prohibit—*v.* to not allow; to forbid. Laws are basically created to <u>prohibit</u> bad behavior like drunk driving and stealing.

prosecute—*v.* to bring a legal case against someone. Famous people are always getting <u>prosecuted</u> for breaking the law. Puff Daddy got <u>prosecuted</u> for carrying an illegal weapon and bribing people to say it wasn't his. Jennifer Lopez was with him when he got arrested, but she didn't get <u>prosecuted</u>. I wonder why?

prosperity—*n.* success and riches. America is known for being a land of <u>prosperity</u>—there are a lot of people in this country who are rich and middle class. Many countries have no <u>prosperity</u> at all—everyone is poor.

provoke—*v.* to anger; to egg on. Many animals are quite peaceful until they are <u>provoked</u>. Most bears won't even pay you any attention, but if you <u>provoke</u> them by poking them with a stick, you are in big trouble.

public domain—*n.* land that's owned by the state or government instead of by a person. Theoretically, that means all taxpayers "own" and can use the land. In the West, a lot of livestock graze on land that's <u>public domain</u>.

qualifications—*n.* skills. A person needs only two <u>qualifications</u> to be president of the United States—to be born in the United States and to be over 35 years old. That's it.

radical—*n.* someone who works for political or social revolution. Our country has a complicated relationship with <u>radicals</u>. When we were colonies breaking from England, we were the <u>radicals</u>, breaking the law. Now, as the most powerful nation in the world, we generally look down on <u>radicals</u>. And as a country based on the rule of law, revolution is not really our cup of tea. Just look at the famous <u>radicals</u> our country has had to see how complicated our relationship with them is.

ratify—*v.* to pass. After a law is written, it has to be <u>ratified</u> by both houses of Congress—the House of Representatives and the Senate, before it is signed (or vetoed) by the president.

ration—*v.* to give out in restricted amounts, usually during wartime, to conserve resources. Food and fuel are often <u>rationed</u> during wartime so more resources can be devoted to fighting the battles.

rational—*adj.* reasonable. If I think <u>rationally</u>, I know it's more important to get a great education than it is to surf all day and try to turn pro.

rebellion—*n.* a revolt against authority. Have you noticed how many words there are in this section that basically mean "revolt" and "<u>rebel</u>"? It is an important subject when it comes to the history of our country. Not only was <u>rebellion</u> how the United States broke from England, <u>rebels</u> have qualities that we as Americans value—<u>rebels</u> do what they think is right, no matter what anyone thinks.

Reconstruction—*n.* the period after the Civil War when the South was controlled by the federal government, before those states were readmitted to the Union (1865-1877).

reform—*v.* to change for the better. One of the great things about our government is that if a law—or the government— doesn't work, we can <u>reform</u> it by voting for representatives who want to change things, too.

regional—*adj.* area-specific. I surf in <u>regional</u> tournaments a few times a year. How well I do in <u>regionals</u> determines if I make it to the year-end national tournament in Hawaii.

regulate—*v.* to control. The government <u>regulates</u> all kinds of things. The most important may be the toxic emissions from cars and power plants. The government <u>regulates</u> the poisons in those emissions by setting limits the companies must not exceed. If a company doesn't follow those <u>regulations,</u> it gets fined.

Related **Word**

regulation—n.
a rule restricting
behavior or actions.

relative—*adj.* in comparison. For example, <u>relative</u> to Shaquille O'Neal, I am a tiny bug. But <u>relative</u> to a tiny bug, I am a huge skyscraper.

repeal—*v.* to take back; to rescind. Sometimes a law is <u>repealed</u> because is was really a bad, bad idea. One of the reasons the colonies broke from England was that England wouldn't <u>repeal</u> tax laws that were really hard on the colonies.

representation—*n.* the act of standing for something or someone. In the phrase "taxation without <u>representation</u>," it means not having <u>representatives</u> in the government looking out for your interests. The main reason the colonies broke with England was that they were being taxed, but had no say at all in how much they were taxed and why.

repress—*n.* to hold back. My dad said the history of man can be seen as a history of <u>repression</u>. Those in power do their best to <u>repress</u> those who aren't, until those who aren't in power get sick of it and revolt. Then they are in power, and then they start <u>repressing</u> some other people! It never stops, according to my dad.

republic—*n.* a government where the people elect representatives to do their bidding. The United States is a <u>republic</u>. Texas used to be its own <u>republic</u> before it became part of the United States.

Antonym

monarchy—n.
a government
ruled by a king
or queen.

resolute—*adj.* firm; unwavering. I am <u>resolute</u> in my view that the Dodgers are the best team in baseball, no matter what their actual record is.

responsibilities—*n.* duties; things you have to do. As citizens of the United States, we have a ton of rights, but we also have a ton of <u>responsibilities</u>. Those include being tolerant of one another; helping those less fortunate than ourselves; obeying the laws meant to protect everyone equally; and driving on the right side of the road, not the left.

restrain—*v.* to hold back. For example, in American history, the New England <u>Restraining</u> Act was enacted by King Charles II in 1775. It <u>restrained</u> a handful of colonies from trading with anyone, and it made those colonies mad.

retaliation—*n.* the act of striking back after you get attacked. It is not good to start a fight, but sometimes <u>retaliation</u> is necessary. Lincoln issued the Order of <u>Retaliation</u> in 1863 saying that if the South violated the rules of war by killing or enslaving captured Union soldiers, the Union would <u>retaliate</u> by doing the same to their soldiers.

Ant🟊onym
surrender—v.
to give up.

revenue—*n.* money made. Government gets its revenue from taxes. Companies get their <u>revenue</u> by selling things. I get my <u>revenue</u> from my allowance and mowing lawns.

samurai—*n.* a Japanese knight. <u>Samurai</u> were expected to be courageous, honorable, and loyal.

secede—*v.* to break away from a unit. The South <u>seceded</u> from the United States in 1861. That's what started the Civil War, because President Lincoln would not let them do it without a fight. The South's <u>secession</u> was a pivotal moment in this country's history.

secular—*adj.* not pertaining to religion. The United States has a <u>secular</u> government, but religion is still a big part of many citizens' personal lives. The framers of the Constitution wanted to keep church and state separate.

sedition—*n.* words or deeds causing people to rebel against the state. During wartime, acts of <u>sedition</u> are not tolerated. In 1798, the U.S. Congress passed the Alien and <u>Sedition</u> Acts to prevent political dissidents and the press from interfering with preparations for war with France.

Ant🟊onym
integration—n. the
combining of
groups of people.

segregation—*n.* the separation of people who are different. Blacks were <u>segregated</u> from white society for years in this country. In some churches, women and men are <u>segregated</u>, with women sitting on one side, men on the other. Boys are often <u>segregated</u> from girls in gym class. <u>Segregation</u> keeps people apart.

shogun—*n.* a Japanese military leader. Technically, the <u>shogun</u> were ruled by the emperor, but the <u>shogun</u> controlled the military, so they had a lot of power.

siege—*n.* in war, a sustained attack. In World War I, troops were under a continuous state of <u>siege</u>. The fighting never stopped as the soldiers on both sides dug trenches and refused to give an inch.

sovereign—*n.* a king or queen. We don't have any <u>sovereigns</u> in our country. England still has its <u>sovereigns</u>, but they don't have any power anymore. They are just symbols of England's past.

subversive—*adj.* undermining. As part of preparing for a war against France, Thomas Jefferson signed the Alien and Sedition Acts, which outlawed <u>subversive</u> behavior, like criticizing the government. Now we can criticize the government as much as we want.

succession—*n.* the process of following in order. There has been a <u>succession</u> of kings and queens in the history of most European nations. Sometimes the <u>succession</u> went smoothly. Sometimes, it was bloody.

suffrage—*n.* the right to vote. Women gained <u>suffrage</u> in this country in 1920. Eighteen-year-olds gained <u>suffrage</u> after the Vietnam War when they argued that if they could go to war, why couldn't they vote?

surplus—*n.* left-overs. You have probably heard of the federal government's budget <u>surplus</u>. That's the money left over after the government uses the taxes we pay to pay its bills.

sympathizers—*n.* people who agree with something and want to help; people who are sympathetic to a person or a cause. Usually in American history, the word is used in the term "communist <u>sympathizers</u>," which means people who agreed with the communists and helped them out in the early 20th century.

tariff—*n.* tax on imports and exports. High <u>tariffs</u> on the colonies' imports and exports made colonists mad at England. You know what happened next.

temperance—*n.* the act of not drinking alcohol. There was a <u>temperance</u> movement in the United States in the early 20th century that made drinking alcohol illegal. That was when gangsters like Al Capone made millions selling illegal booze.

transcend—*v.* to surpass; to overcome. Sometimes you have to <u>transcend</u> your limitations to reach your goals. If your vocabulary is a limitation for you, this book should help you <u>transcend</u> that obstacle.

tripartite—*adj.* divided into three parts. We have a <u>tripartite</u> federal government consisting of the executive, legislative, and judicial branches.

truce—*n.* a stop in the fighting. Sometimes in a war the sides just call a <u>truce</u> without anyone declaring victory. They just stop fighting because they are tired of seeing their people killed.

tyranny—*n.* total power used in a cruel way. Once I accused the judges at surfing regionals of practicing <u>tyranny</u>. I thought they were giving me low marks on a whim, just because they could, because they had all the power. It made them mad.

unanimous—*adj.* being in complete, 100 percent agreement. In a <u>unanimous</u> decision, everyone votes the same way. When we took a vote from the students at school about our dress code, the students voted <u>unanimously</u> to repeal it.

urban—*adj.* related to the city. Lots of big cities around the country have been undergoing <u>urban</u> renewal, which means they are working to improve the quality of their inner cities and downtown areas.

To remember subversive means "undermining" remember sub means "under."

To remember suffrage, remember people "suffer" when they don't have the right to vote.

Antonym
deficit—n. the amount something comes up short.

WhizQuiz
Name a limitation you have had to transcend in your life:
_____

Related Word
majority—adj. In a majority vote, more than 50 percent of the people vote one way, but not everybody.

rural—adj. related to the countryside.

39

usurp—*v.* to take over; to seize power. Many times members of Congress have tried to <u>usurp</u> the authority of the president by passing legislation that lessens the president's power. Sometimes they have prevailed, sometimes they have failed. Once I tried to <u>usurp</u> my parents and told my sister she could stay up late when they told her she had to go to sleep. I got in trouble for that one.

Whiz Tip

Fruitopia is a fruit drink that plays off the word utopia: Fruitopia is supposed to be the "perfect" fruit drink.

utopia—*n.* a perfect world. Many systems of government promise their followers a <u>utopia</u> on Earth. I think Hawaii is the closest anyone has come to <u>utopia</u> yet!

verdict—*n.* a decision in a court case. It is the job of a jury to reach a <u>verdict</u> in a case. When members of a jury don't reach a <u>verdict</u>, it's called a "hung jury."

veteran—*n.* someone who has fought in a war. We celebrate <u>Veterans</u> Day to remember the people who have fought in all of our wars. My great-grandfather is a <u>veteran</u>—he fought in World War II.

veto—*n.* rejection of a proposal. In our government, a <u>veto</u> is a president's vote against legislation passed by Congress. Presidents often <u>veto</u> legislation they don't agree with.

Antonym

mandatory—**adj.** forced.

voluntary—*adj.* of one's own choice, with no outside force. Our armed forces are now <u>voluntary</u>, but in times of war, you can be forced to fight. At my school, joining band or sports is <u>voluntary</u>, but everyone must take math and science.

WhizWords
communism
democracy
despotism
fascism
federalism
imperialism
republic

History-Social Science

Government

I was over at my great-grandfather's assisted living complex the other day, and he was going on and on about World War II. He's a good guy, but when you get him started on World War II, you might as well pull up a chair because you're going to be there for a while. Anyway, he was talking about **fascism** and **communism** and all of these different kinds of governments I have only heard of in history class.

It made me realize that I wrongly assumed that all countries are **democracies** like ours. When my great-grandfather was growing up, Germany had a **fascist** government; Russia was part of the Soviet Union and was a **communist** country; **imperialism** was the favorite kind of government for all kinds of kings in the Middle East; and the African countries that weren't run as colonies by France and England were run by **despots**.

My great-grandfather lived in crazy times! Today, the Middle East oil countries are still pretty much all run by kings, and Africa is still full of **despots**, but lots of the rest of the countries—like Germany and Japan—have gone **democratic**.

Related Word

nationalism—n. You really like your country, and hate all the other countries. Nazi Germany was based on intense nationalism. The Nazis were going to rule the whole world, and kill anyone they thought was unworthy of being a member of the Third Reich.

IDENTIFY THE GOVERNMENT TYPE EXERCISE

Following are some countries that have gone through some big changes over the years. If you don't know what kind of government was in place on the dates I give you (and from the hints in my descriptions), do some research in the library or on the Internet to find out. You will be very surprised by what you find.

Country	Year	Government?
England	1714	King George I assumes the throne.
Texas	1836	Texas is an independent republic.
United States	1897	William McKinley was elected our 25th president.
Germany	1935	Hitler rules with an iron fist.
Jordan	1953	King Hussein assumes his hereditary position.
Cambodia	1976	The totalitarian Khmer Rouge wreak havoc.
England	1979	Margaret Thatcher is elected England's first woman prime minister.

Whenever you hear about a country in the news that you don't know anything about, do some research and figure out what kind of government it has. I've been doing this for the last few months whenever I hear about a country in Africa or Asia, because I don't know very much about those two continents. It is really scary how few democracies there are out there!

WhizWords

anarchy
insurgent
insurrection
militant
radical
rebellion
subversive

History-Social Science
Revolution

Related **Word**

utopia—n. a
perfect world.
Many rebellions
are led by
radicals who
promise their
followers utopia.

Rebellion is a tricky subject. Whether a revolution is good or bad often depends on which side you are on. For example, the colonists' **rebellion** against mother England is the only reason the United States of America even exists. And our democracy was a big experiment at the time. The fact that it worked basically opened the door for democracies everywhere. So there—a "good" **insurrection.**

But if you watch the news every day, you see **revolutions** all over the place, and they are not pretty, and the result of the **rebellion** is not always good.

THE HISTORY OF REBELLION EXERCISE
From our history and the continuing events in many countries, you can see why words about rebellion and revolution are so important to know. To get a better handle on the vocabulary often used to describe revolution and revolutionaries, I want you to write one short essay comparing and contrasting any two rebellions. For your convenience, I'll go ahead and list some of the more interesting rebellions of the past few hundred years:

   1. 1776: Colonists Rebel Against England
   2. 1789: The French rebel against King Louis XVI
   3. 1917: Russians rebel against the czar
   4. 1956: Communists in Cuba revolt

Be sure to use all of the "Revolution" words in the essay, and try to squeeze in the Related Word as well. If, when you have completed your exercise, you want to make sure you are comfortable with the words, compare two of the remaining rebellions to test yourself.

Related **Word**

sympathizer—n.
a person who agrees
with a cause
and wants to help.
A sympathizer might
participate in
subversive activities
to support a
radical cause.

WhizWords
abolitionist
bias
discriminate
emancipation
feminism
integration
intolerant
oppress
persecute
segregation
suffrage

History-Social Science
Inequality

People rebel because they feel they are being **oppressed** or **discriminated** against. **Feminists** fight for the rights of women every day because women don't have the same rights as men. **Abolitionists** fought for the freedom of slaves, who didn't have any rights at all. In fact, the history of our country is filled with situations where individuals had to overcome **bias**. It was once common to **discriminate** based on race and gender. And our country is called the land of the free! So you can just imagine what life is like in countries where equality isn't even talked about, much less strived for.

In the United States, we have made great strides. There is pretty much universal **suffrage** now—everyone over the age of 18 can vote. Our public schools, public places, and the military are all **integrated**, too. **Segregation** used to keep black people separated from white people.

Even so, there is still a lot of **intolerance** around. Lots of the advances in equality have happened in the past 20 or 30 years, but old habits die hard. So some people still use stereotypes to judge those who are different than they are.

Related Word

diversity—n. variety. Diversity and integration can help people learn that stereotypes and biases are shallow and stupid.

• •

SUFFRAGE FOR FASHION MODELS EXERCISE

The fight for equal rights is a serious business. People have given their lives so that others might have equal opportunity. However, for this exercise, let's lighten things up a little. Pretend there is only one group left in this country that is being discriminated against: skinny fashion models. Now, get a pencil and paper and write a make-believe history about how skinny fashion models go from being segregated, discriminated against, and not having the right to vote, to being integrated, having equal rights, and having suffrage in the year 2050. Use as many of the words above as you can.

ESSAY:

The History of Skinny Fashion Models' Fight
For Suffrage in the 21st Century

WhizWords

ambition
carpetbagger
civic
impeachment
inaugurate
lame duck
mandate
partisan

History-Social Science

Politics

WhizTip

The best way to build your vocabulary is to read, read, and read some more. Newspapers are a good source of reading material. You'll find new information about things you're interested in every day.

Did you pay attention to the 2000 presidential race? When it started I didn't pay too much attention. But my dad is such a big Al Gore fan, he made me go to some rallies, and I started to get excited. And then the election! Nobody won! It took them about a month to figure out who the next president was going to be. It was the first time I stopped thinking about surfing and started thinking about something else outside of school.

The election got me started reading the political stories in the newspaper. That's when I started to realize there was a ton of words I didn't know very well. For example—**carpetbagger.** Have you ever heard that word? And **lame duck.** I mean, what do ducks have to do with politics, especially ducks that waddle with a limp?

Apparently a lot, because **lame duck** and **carpetbagger** kept coming up over and over again, along with **impeachment, mandate,** and **partisan.** It's no wonder they are important to know for tests. If you know these words, you will be a more informed citizen, and, therefore, probably vote for the right person more often. At least that's the idea.

READ THE POLITICS PAGE EXERCISE
Keep this book handy. Pick up the latest copy of your local newspaper. Not the free handout you get at the grocery store with all of the used cars for sale—the real thing. Start with the Sunday paper if you can—it's usually about twice as thick. Now find the stories about local and national politics and start reading. Whenever you see one of the WhizWords above, underline it. Write down the number of times each word appears.

Keep doing this for one week. That's right—read the political stories every day for one week. People may think you are crazy, but do it anyway. You can still read the sports page and the comics (my personal favorites), but read political news first. Underline, count, write the "Politics" words listed above in this chart.

	Day 1	Day 2	Day 3	Day 4	Day 5	Day 6	Day 7
ambition							
carpetbagger							
civic							
impeachment							
inaugurate							
lame duck							
mandate							
partisan							

Which word won? Which came in second? Make sure you know the Top Three like the back of your hand, and make sure you know the rest of 'em like the front of your hand.

WhizWords

boom and bust economy
capital
capitalist
commerce
commodity
economy
entrepreneur
free enterprise
profit
surplus

History-Social Science

Economics

Did I say this country was all about freedom and equality? Just ask Alex Rodriguez, who signed a contract with the Texas Rangers for over $250 million, what this country is all about, and he might say "Show me the money!"

I mean, I love Alex Rodriguez. He is definitely one of the best shortstops in the league. But $250 million? I think he gets like $50,000 for each at bat or something like that. I only get $10 a week for my allowance! Maybe Alex can spare a few hundred bucks?

No wonder tests ask so many questions about **economics** and **capitalism.** As a citizen of the richest country on the planet, it is important that you know how **capitalism** works so you can carry on the tradition. Especially if you end up being Alex Rodriguez!

READ THE BUSINESS PAGE EXERCISE

This exercise is basically a repeat of the politics exercise. After you get done with your week of reading the political stories in the paper, I want you to do a week of reading the business stories in the paper. I know—and you thought it couldn't get any more boring than politics!

Here's your chart for the week:

	Day 1	Day 2	Day 3	Day 4	Day 5	Day 6	Day 7
boom and bust							
capital							
capitalist							
commerce							
commodity							
economy							
entrepreneur							
free enterprise							
profit							
surplus							

Again, know the Top Three like the back of your hand and the rest like the front of your hand.

Chapter 3

Math

angle—*n.* the figure formed when two lines meet at a point. There are three kinds of <u>angles</u>: *acute* (less than 90°), *obtuse* (greater than 90°), and *right* (90°).

acute angle

obtuse angle

right angle

angle—*n.* oh yeah, there are two more kinds of angles—complementary and supplementary. <u>Complementary angles</u> add up to 90°. <u>Supplementary angles</u> add up to 180°.

WhizFact

π **is a decimal that never repeats. You can round it off at 3.14 if you need to estimate a circumference or area.**

area—*n.* the amount of surface on a figure. For example, a rectangle's <u>area</u> is length x width. A triangle's <u>area</u> is 1/2 base x height. A circle's <u>area</u> is πr^2. Just remember: <u>area</u> is the amount of space inside the lines.

average—*n.* what you get when you add up a bunch of numbers and then divide by the number of numbers you added up. The <u>average</u> of the numbers 9, 13, 28, 72, 83 = (9 + 13 + 28 + 72 + 83) ÷ 5 = 205 ÷ 5 = 41. So 41 is the <u>average</u> of those five numbers.

axiom—*n.* an established rule.

DOUBLE MEANING

average—*adj.* nothing special, middle-of-the-road, normal.

bisect—*v.* to divide into two usually equal parts. In math, a line or a point usually <u>bisects</u> another line. It cuts that line into two parts. Once in science we had to dissect a frog, and I had to <u>bisect</u> its brain—I actually cut its brain in half. I almost fainted.

capacity—*n.* the amount something can hold. For example, my dad's Nissan Stanza's gas tank has a <u>capacity</u> of 12 gallons of gas.

circumference—*n.* the length of the boundary of a circle. If you took a circle and straightened out the line that surrounds it and measured it, that's the <u>circumference</u>. The formula to find a circle's <u>circumference</u> is $2\pi r$, with *r* standing for *radius*.

congruent—*adj.* having the same shape and size. If you put one <u>congruent</u> shape on top of the other, they would be exactly the same. In math, this is most often used to describe <u>congruent</u> triangles.

consecutive—*adj.* occurring in order, one right after the other. In math, it is most often used to describe <u>consecutive</u> numbers in a number pattern. Players also talk about how hard it is to play on <u>consecutive</u> days in sports like baseball and basketball because they don't get to rest between games.

constant—*n.* an element in a math problem that doesn't change. π is an example of a <u>constant</u>—it never changes.

convert—*v.* to change from one system of measurement to another. Most often used when <u>converting</u> our system of measurements to the metric system. See the measurements page at the end of this section for some common measurements and <u>conversions</u>.

converge—*v.* to come together at a point. Lines <u>converge</u>. So do rivers. In Pennsylvania, the Allegheny and Monongahela rivers <u>converge</u> to form the Ohio River.

coordinates—*n.* a set of two numbers that shows where a point goes on a coordinate plane.

data—*n.* facts and figures; the information you are given in a math problem. Test questions are always asking you to look at the <u>data</u> and answer the question.

denominator—*n.* the number under the line in a fraction.

diagonal—*n.* in a rectangle, a line slanting from one corner to the other. The "Diver Down" flag used by scuba divers has a diagonal line across it—that's a good way to get a visual of the word <u>diagonal</u>.

diameter—*n.* the length across the middle of a circle. If you are given the radius of the circle, double it to get the <u>diameter</u>: $d = 2r$

digit—*n.* 1, 2, 3, 4, 5, 6, 7, 8, 9, and 0 are digits. Math problems are always using two-<u>digit</u> numbers (also called tens: 23, 61), three-<u>digit</u> numbers (also called hundreds: 154, 982), and four-<u>digit</u> numbers (also called thousands:1,468).

dimensions—*n.* the length, width, and/or height of an object. Geometric shapes have <u>dimensions</u>, houses have <u>dimensions</u>, football fields have <u>dimensions</u>. Pretty much everything you can see has <u>dimensions</u>.

dividend—*n.* a number divided by another number. In the math problem 64 ÷ 6, 64 is the <u>dividend</u> (6 is the divisor).

Whiz Quiz

Pick the next number in these number patterns:
3, 6, 9, 12, __
–3, –1, 1, 3, __
3/4, 1 1/2, 2 1/4, __

DOUBLE MEANING
convert—v.
to change from one religion or set of beliefs to another (history-social science).

coordinates

diagonal

47

Math

DOUBLE MEANING
domain—*n.*
territory ruled
by a king or queen
(history-social
science).

On the Test
List all of the
factors for 72.

Bar Graph

Circle Graph
(Pie Graph)

Whiz Quiz
Circle the integers.
1/2
.6
6
–6
–2
0
3.2
6.9
3/4
17
–12
243
–55/3

48

divisor—*n.* the number that divides another number. See *dividend*.

domain—*n.* the set of the first coordinates of a group of ordered pairs. (The set of second coordinates is the *range*.)

estimate—*v.* to make a reasonable guess. When a math problem asks you to <u>estimate,</u> it means look at the data and make a guess that makes sense. I <u>estimate</u> things every day—from how long it's going to take to get ready for school to how much trouble I am going to get in for missing the bus because I <u>underestimated</u> how long it would take to get ready for school.

exponent—*n.* a number off to the upper right of another number that shows the power to which the number is raised. That means whatever the <u>exponent</u> is, you multiply a number times itself that many times. $4^3 = 4 \times 4 \times 4 = 64$.

factor—*n.* a number that can be multiplied with others to achieve a product. Hmm. How can I put this. Pick a number. The numbers you multiply to get that number are its <u>factors</u>. Take the number 27, for instance, some of its <u>factors</u> are 3 x 3 x 3 (= 27). Some others are 9 x 3 (= 27). Some others are 27 x 1 (= 27). The number 13 has <u>factors</u> of 13 x 1 (= 13). *Note*: 13 is also a prime number—which means its only <u>factors</u> are itself and 1.

graphs—*n.* you need to know how to read two main kinds of graphs—circle graphs and bar graphs. A <u>circle graph</u> is also called a pie graph. The different sized slices of pie show relative proportions of something, like the amount of attention four brothers and sisters get from their parents. A <u>bar graph</u> measures things on an *x*- and *y*-axis. The *x*-axis stands for one thing (like years) and the *y*-axis stands for another (like height). Note: You may also see <u>line graphs</u> here and there: they look like a jagged mountain top set on an *x*-axis.

horizontal—*adj.* straight across. To remember the word, think of a "horizon."

hypotenuse—*n.* the longest side of a right triangle; the side opposite the 90° angle. About the only time you will see questions about the <u>hypotenuse</u> is in questions about right triangles.

inequality—*n.* an algebraic statement that sets one quantity as greater than or less than another. <u>Inequalities</u> typically use the < (less than) and > (greater than) symbols.

integer—*n.* positive whole numbers, negative whole numbers, and zero are <u>integers</u>. No fractions and no decimals are <u>integers</u>—ever! Think of <u>integers</u> as having too much "integrity" to get involved with messy fractions and decimals.

intersect—*v.* to cross each other. Lines <u>intersect</u> on graphs. To remember it, think of street <u>intersections</u>—where streets cross each other.

intercept—*n.* the place where a line, curve, or surface crosses the axis on a graph.

inverse—*n.* a reciprocal of a quantity. The <u>inverse</u> of 4 is –4 because adding or subtracting makes them 0.

irrational number—*n.* a number that cannot be expressed as a fraction or decimal. Like π, or $\sqrt{2}$. You can put an <u>irrational number</u> on a number line, but you can't express the number precisely, like you can with 1.5 and –3. (See the definition for *rational number* if you don't get it yet.)

lowest common denominator—*n.* the smallest whole number that can be divided evenly by the denominators of two fractions. For example, the <u>lowest common denominator</u> for 1/4 and 1/5 is 20. To add 1/4 + 1/5 you must convert them to 5/20 (from 1/4) and 4/20 (from 1/5).

mean—*n.* see the definition for *average*; they are the same thing.

median—*n.* in a group of numbers, it is the one in the middle or the average of the two numbers in the middle. *Example*: Here is a group of numbers: 23, 31, 67, 78, 86, 165, 254. The <u>median</u> is 78—it is the middle number in this series.

mode—*n.* in a group of numbers, it is the number that occurs most often. *Example*: Here is a group of numbers: 23, 24, 24, 25, 26, 27, 28, 29, 29, 30, 31, 32, 32, 32, 33, 34. The <u>mode</u> is 32. It occurs three times—the most of any number in this series.

negative number—*n.* a number less than zero indicated by a minus sign (–). On a number line, the numbers to the left of 0 are <u>negative numbers</u>.

numerator—*n.* the number that is divided by the denominator.

odds—*n.* a ratio of favorable to unfavorable outcomes. For example, what are the <u>odds</u> Kobe Bryant will hit a 20-foot jump shot if he makes four out of every nine 20-footers he takes? The odds are the number of successful attempts over the number of unsuccessful attempts. In this case, 4/5.

order of operations—*n.* the sequence by which you do the operations in an equation. To remember the correct <u>order of operations</u>, think of PEMDAS ("Please Excuse My Dear Aunt Sally"). The <u>order of operations</u> is: parentheses, exponents, multiplication and division, and then addition and subtraction.

parallel—*adj.* relating to lines traveling alongside each other at the same distance without ever touching. Train tracks are <u>parallel</u>.

perimeter—*n.* the outside edge of an object or shape. Think about soldiers patrolling the <u>perimeter</u> of their outpost. That means they are patrolling the edges of their camp, making sure the enemy isn't planning any funny business.

perpendicular—*adj.* relating to lines meeting each other at a right (90⁰) angle. <u>Perpendicular</u> is kind of the opposite of *parallel*. They are mentioned in the same sentence—and the same math problem—all the time.

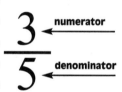

perspective

perspective—*n.* the appearance of depth or three dimensions; when you draw something on a piece of paper, but you give it three dimensions, so it looks like real life. Think about drawing a road that recedes into the distance—the sides of the road get closer together as they go away into the distance. Oh heck, sometimes a picture is worth a thousand words, so just look at the picture of the road on the left. That's <u>perspective</u>.

polygon—*n.* a flat shape with three or more straight sides. A <u>polygon</u> is any shape with flat sides, really, from a triangle to a rectangle to an octagon to whatever a shape with 28 sides is called, and beyond . . . .

Ant·onym

negative
number—n.
a number
less than zero.
The numbers to
the left of 0 on
a number line.

positive number—*n.* a number greater than zero. On a number line, the numbers to the right of 0 are <u>positive numbers</u>.

prime number—*n.* a positive whole number with only itself and one as factors. That means you can't divide any other number into it without getting a remainder. 17 is a <u>prime number</u>. 23 is a <u>prime number</u>. Try all night, you can't divide any other numbers into them without getting a remainder. (See the definition for *factor* in this section for more information.)

probability—*n.* the chance that something will happen, shown as a ratio of favorable outcomes to possible outcomes. For example, if Kobe Bryant hits his 20-foot jump shot four out of every nine times, the probability he will make any given shot is the number of successful attempts over the number of possible attempts. In this case, 4/9.

proportion—*n.* a comparison of equivalent ratios. *Example*: 1/3 = 3/9, which can also be written as 1:3 = 3:9.

Pythagorean theorem—*n.* for right triangles, the sum of the squares of a right triangle's sides is equal to the square of the hypotenuse. $a^2 + b^2 = hyp^2$. (See the definitions for *hypotenuse* and *triangles* for more information.)

quadrilateral—*n.* a four-sided polygon. Squares, rectangles, and rhombuses are all <u>quadrilaterals</u>.

radius—*n.* the line from the center of a circle to its outside edge. The <u>radius</u> is half a circle's diameter.

Related Word

random sample—n.
a group of
numbers or
values chosen
out of the blue.

DOUBLE MEANING

rate—v.
to judge; to rank.

random—*adj.* having no pattern or reason; out of the blue. Lottery numbers are picked at <u>random</u>.

rate—*n.* one thing measured in terms of another thing. Miles per hour. Words per minute. Gallons per flush. Those are all <u>rates</u>.

ratio—*n.* the relationship between two quantities. <u>Ratios</u> can be expressed as fractions (the <u>ratio</u> of four to nine is 4/9) or with a colon (the <u>ratio</u> of six to seven is 6:7).

rational number—*n.* a number that can be expressed as a ratio of two integers. 7 is a <u>rational number</u> (it can be expressed as 7/1). –2/3 is a <u>rational number</u>. 45.4 is a <u>rational number</u>.

reciprocal—*n.* the quotient of a quantity divided into 1. *Example*:

The reciprocal of 1/7 is 7/1. The reciprocal of 6/7 is 7/6.

reflection—*n.* a shape that is flipped, so it's the same, but backwards. Think of it like your reflection in the mirror. All the sides are the same length and the angles are the same size, they are just positioned exactly opposite of where they were.

rotation—*n.* movement in a circular motion around a fixed point. When a geometric shape is rotated, its shape stays the same but the side that was on the bottom may now be on the top.

scale—*n.* when talking about models, scale is the relationship between the size of the model and the size of the real-life object. So if a scale model of an airplane is 1:8, that means the real airplane is eight times as big as the model.

scientific notation—*n.* a way of writing numbers in terms of powers of ten. *Example*: $65,789 = 6.5789 \times 10^4$. $432 = 4.32 \times 10^2$.

sequence—*n.* the order something happens in. In math, it usually means a number sequence, like 2, 4, 6, 8 . . . or a sequence of operations, like performing operations inside parentheses first.

square—*n.* the number you get when you multiply a number by itself. The square of 3 (3 x 3) is 9. The square of 11 (11 x 11) = 121.

square root—*n.* the divisor of a number that when multiplied by itself gives that number. 5 is the square root of 25 because 5^2 (5 x 5) is 25. This can also be expressed as $\sqrt{25} = 5$.

symmetry—*n.* when the stuff on one side of a dividing line matches the stuff on the other. If you draw a line down the middle of your face, the parts on the left match the parts on the right. Your face has symmetry. It is symmetrical. So are some shapes and some graphs.

terminate—*v.* to end; to stop. The word is used in math to describe where decimals terminate. Repeating decimals never terminate—they repeat forever. To remember it, think of the musclebound actor Arnold Schwarzenegger. He played a cyborg in *Terminator*, and he "ended" any puny little people who got in his way.

theorem—*n.* in math, a proposition that is provable. (See the definition of *Pythagorean theorem* for an example.)

three-dimensional—*adj.* having three dimensions, which gives an object depth. Any real object is three-dimensional. Also written as 3-D.

triangle—*n.* a shape with three sides and three angles. There are four kinds of triangles you need to know:

equilateral   **All sides and angles are equal.**

isosceles   **Two sides and their opposite angles are equal.**

On the Test

Express your answer in scientific notation and as a decimal.

Please square these numbers:
2
45
–3
–41
7
–6

Symmetry

Math

right

One angle is 90°. The side opposite the 90° angle is the hypotenuse.

scalene

All sides and angles are different from each other.

Whiz Quiz

Solve the
following
problems with
the variables
x=2 and *y*=3

2*x*
4*y*
–5*y*
x – *y*
2*y* + 7*x*
–2*x* – 4*y*

two-dimensional—*adj.* having two dimensions, which means the object has no depth (it resides on a single plane). Also written as 2-D.

variable—*n.* a symbol whose value can change. In math, the variable is usually called *x* or *y*. That means you can plug in different numbers for the variable *x* or *y* or *z* or whatever. To remember the word, think of watching a weather report. The weatherman often says that "winds are variable," and weather itself is always variable (changing).

vertical—*adj.* going straight up and down. Like a flag pole.

volume—*n.* the amount of space something occupies. You can get Coca-Cola in all kinds of different volumes, from a 12-ounce can to a 16-ounce bottle to a three-liter bottle. I prefer the three-liter bottle.

whole number—*n.* an integer. Positive or negative. Not a fraction, not a decimal, not an irrational number. Just nice, clean integers are whole numbers.

Math
Measurements Page

METRIC AND
BRITISH IMPERIAL MEASUREMENTS

Measurement conversion charts are provided on most math tests, so it's important you know how to read them. Measuring is the only time I wish I was European. They have things so easy when it comes to measuring. As you probably know, their metric system is all based on tens. Anyway, here are the measurements that are used most often on tests—in metric and British Imperial (that's what we use). Don't ask me why we use British Imperial and the English use metrics. Because I don't know.

BRITISH IMPERIAL
Distance

Foot	12 inches
Yard	3 feet
Mile	1,760 yards

Volume

Pint	16 ounces
Quart	2 pints
Gallon	4 quarts

Weight

Pound	16 ounces
Ton	2,000 pounds

METRIC
Distance

Centimeter	10 millimeters
Meter	100 centimeters
Kilometer	1,000 meters

Volume

Liter	1,000 milliliters

Weight

Gram	1,000 milligrams
Kilogram	1,000 grams
Metric ton	1,000 kilograms

COMMON CONVERSIONS
(ALL CONVERSIONS ARE APPROXIMATE)
Distance

BRITISH IMPERIAL	METRIC
Inch	about 3 centimeters
Yard	about 1 meter
Mile	about 1.6 kilometers

Volume

BRITISH IMPERIAL	METRIC
Ounce	about 29 milliliters
Cup	about 1/4 liter
Gallon	about 3.79 liters

Weight

BRITISH IMPERIAL	METRIC
Ounce	about 29 grams
Pound	about 450 grams
	(about 1/2 kilogram)

53

Exercises

WhizWords

denominator
numerator
ratio

Math

Ratios

The great thing about situation comedies is that they are kind of the same every week. The jokes change, the wacky, far-fetched situations change, but the characters and the settings remain the same. Unless, of course, a show decides to take its characters on a whirlwind European vacation to boost ratings during sweeps week.

In fact, you can almost predict how many times a certain character is going to do a certain thing. For example, on the show *Friends*, my sister and I play this game guessing how many times the character Rachel will touch her hair while she's talking. Last week I guessed 23. I was close—it was 27. Unfortunately, my sister guessed 26, so she won and I had to do the dishes for her the next day.

SITUATION COMEDY RATIOS EXERCISE

For this exercise you need a pencil and paper to keep track of things. You can play this one alone, but it is more fun if you have a friend or relative to compete with. First, pick a TV show. For this example, I'll use the show *Malcolm in the Middle*. Second, pick something to count. My friend Larry and I picked: How many times Malcolm's bullying brother Reese is in a scene, and how many times he hits Malcolm, or anyone else for that matter. Put these in two columns. Third, predict how many times you think each will occur and write that down. Fourth, start counting. Use hash marks to keep track, and when the show is over, tally up your totals.

Reese in scene	Reese smacks someone
Les—24	Les—6
Larry—19	Larry—7
Actual—23	Actual—3

Compute the ratios for your guesses.

What is the ratio of Reese hits vs. Reese appearances?

Les	6 : 24
Larry	7 : 19
Actual	3 : 23

Answer additional questions using the data you have amassed. What are the ratios expressed as fractions? What is the numerator in Larry's ratio? What is the denominator in Larry's ratio?

<u>Extra Credit</u>: Watch the same TV show three times and do this exercise three times. After the three shows, compare the ratios from show to show. How much do they vary?

54

Circles

So you need more proof that math is all around you? Fine. Let's talk about circles. Circles are obviously everywhere, from the portholes on a ship to the circles under your parents' eyes. The invention of the wheel, the hardest working circle of all time, was a big event, right up there with the invention of Pop Rocks and Napster.

Of course on math tests, you have to do a little more than just appreciate the importance of roundness. You have to be able to calculate **diameters** and **circumferences** of circles of all sizes.

DIFFERENT SIZE CIRCLES EXERCISE
I have given you a variety of circles below. I want you to find the circumference and diameter of each. I'm even going to help you out a bit. Here are the equations for each:

Diameter = 2r

Circumference = 2πr

Note: Circles not drawn to scale.

Now, get a ruler. Go and find five more circles in your house and measure the radius—that's half the diameter. Use those measurements to find the diameter and the circumference of the circles you found. Don't know where to start? Try the kitchen, the home of circular housewares.

Note: π is the ratio of the circumference of a circle to its diameter. The actual value for π is approximately 3.14159.

WhizWords

integer
irrational number
negative number
positive number
prime number
rational number
whole number

Math
Number Types

Still not convinced of math's importance in your everyday existence? I was like you once, before I saw the light. One part of math you can't dispute is that numbers are everywhere. We measure ingredients, tell time, and count the days until summer vacation.

What you probably don't do while you are counting the days to summer vacation is think about what kind of number you have in your head. The "31" in "31 days until summer vacation" is an **integer**, a **positive number**, a **prime number**, a **rational number**, and a **whole number**. Those are the kinds of things you need to know for math tests. So let's review.

NUMBERS YOU SEE EVERY DAY EXERCISE

Label each of the numbers with all of the number types from above that match. If none match, write "none." I'll do the first couple so you get the idea.

17 years old   integer, positive number, prime number, rational number, whole number

–3 degrees   integer, negative number, rational number, whole number

$.79 Snickers bar   _____

.327 batting average   _____

2 1/2 weeks   _____

4 hours   _____

–12 under par   _____

A drink coaster with a circumference _____
of 6π (okay, I'm stretching here) _____

Math
Number Relationships

Whether you believe that math affects your everyday life or not, you still have to take tests about it. One thing that shows up on all sorts of math tests is number relationships. Questions about number relationships usually involve a long lists of numbers and ask you to figure out the **mean**, **median,** or **mode**. Sometimes all three.

Just remember:
- **mean** (means average)
- **median** (in the middle of the road)
- **mode** (sounds like most)

So let's get to it.

TEST GRADES EXERCISE
Find the mean, median, and mode of my grades last year on tests in English-Language Arts, math, science, and history.

		Mean	Median	Mode
English	56, 92, 87, 79, 95, 92, 99			
Math	78, 82, 91, 79, 78, 97, 93			
Science	94, 91, 99, 100, 89, 94, 94			
Social Science	102, 84, 72, 67, 84, 94, 84			

Find the mean, median, and mode of these three baseball players' batting averages over their careers.

		Mean	Median	Mode
Paul O'Neill	.333, .256, .252, .276, .270, .256, .246, .311, .359, .300, .302, .324, .317, .285, .283			
Manny Ramirez	.269, .308, .309, .328, .294, .333, .351			
Alex Rodriguez	.232, .358, .300, .310, .285, .316			
Derek Jeter	.314, .291, .324, .349, .339			
Tony Gwynn	.289, .309, .351, .317, .329, .370, .313, .336, .309, .317, .317, .358, .394, .368, .353, .372, .321, .338, .323			

For more practice, line up your grades from last semester or last year and find the mean, median, and mode.

Chapter 4

Science

absorb—*v.* to soak up. Commercials for paper towels brag about how they <u>absorb</u> spills. You have probably heard your teacher say that she hopes you are <u>absorbing</u> everything she says.

acclimatization—*n.* adaptation to changes in climates. It took a while for the <u>acclimatization</u> of my new pet snake to its new aquarium. It didn't eat for a week!

adhere—*v.* to stick to. Scotch tape <u>adheres</u> to paper quite well. It does not <u>adhere</u> to running water.

artery—*n.* a blood vessel carrying blood from the heart.

asteroids—*n.* a bunch of big rocks orbiting the sun, kind of like mini-planets. Most <u>asteroids</u> are in between the planets Mars and Jupiter. In sci-fi movies, space ships are always getting caught up in <u>asteroid</u> belts. Just remember, they are called "belts" because they are "wrapping around" the sun.

atmosphere—*n.* the layer of gases surrounding the Earth or another planet. The Earth's <u>atmosphere</u> is mostly oxygen and nitrogen.

atom—*n.* the smallest unit of an element that has all the properties of that element. Everything in the world is made up of <u>atoms</u>. The <u>atom</u> bomb gets its power from when <u>atoms</u> are split—that's how much energy is stored up in this tiny little particle. It's kind of scary when you think about it.

bacteria—*n.* one-celled organisms. They are all around us, but you can't see them. My mom buys anti-<u>bacterial</u> soap because she thinks me and my sister are getting too many colds—she thinks it's because of all the <u>bacteria</u> on our hands.

beneficial—*adj.* helpful; good. Learning the words in this book should prove to be <u>beneficial</u> to your grades. Hey, it can't hurt!

biomass—*n.* all of the living things in an environment. The *mass* of *bio*—get it?

biotic—*adj.* of or pertaining to life. You can remember this word by thinking of *antibiotic*, which is supposed to *kill* whatever microorganisms are living inside your body.

buoyant—*adj.* it floats! Ivory soap is <u>buoyant</u>, but Zest and Irish Spring sink like stones.

capillary—*n.* an itty bitty blood vessel that attaches small veins to small arteries. If you are looking at a road map, the superhighways are

Related Word

vein—n. veins carry blood back to the heart from the body.

DOUBLE MEANING

atmosphere—n. the atmosphere is like the mood in a story—it's a writer's tool (English-language arts).

WhizTip

To remember beneficial, think of people giving benefits for charitable causes. That's a good thing to do.

major veins and arteries, the state highways are smaller veins and arteries, and the little roads and streets connecting the state highways are capillaries.

carbon—*n*. the element found in all living things. One of the ways scientists find the age of a fossil is to use carbon dating. That's when they measure how much carbon is left in a fossil and calculate how old that makes it.

carnivore—*n*. meat-eater. The most ferocious carnivore known to mice is the house cat.

catalyst—*n*. in science, a substance that speeds up a chemical reaction without being changed itself. Fire is a catalyst for turning water into evaporated water (steam).

catastrophic—*adj*. tragic and awful, causing great pain and suffering. I hope Kobe Bryant doesn't suffer a catastrophic injury to his knee. That would ruin the Lakers' season.

categorize—*v*. to divide up into groups. When my dad does the laundry, he always categorizes the clothes as whites and colors. I, on the other hand, just throw everything in together.

celestial—*adj*. related to the stars and the universe. Planets and asteroids and suns and stuff are all called "celestial bodies."

cell—*n*. the smallest, most basic part of any living thing. A cell is filled with protoplasm, has a nucleus near its center, and has a membrane that keeps it all together.

centrifugal force—*n*. moving away from the center. When you swing a bucket of water around in a circle real fast, and the water doesn't fall out, that's centrifugal force!

chain reaction—*n*. a series of events in which one thing leads to another, which leads to another. I saw a chain reaction accident on the highway once when a semi jackknifed, and all of the cars behind it ran into each other.

chloroplast—*n*. the part of a plant cell that contains the chlorophyll.

chromosome—*n*. the part of the cell that carries an organism's DNA (which determines its hereditary characteristics).

circulatory system—*n*. the organs that move blood around the body, including the heart, veins, arteries, and capillaries. Just think of

DOUBLE MEANING
catalyst—**n. someone who makes things happen. Usually used in history when talking about a movement or revolution. The feminist movement's leader, Gloria Steinem, was a catalyst for change for women in the 1960s.**

Antonym
centripetal force—**n. moving toward a center. It's what keeps the planets orbiting around the sun.**

Science

the pipes and plumbing that circulate water in your house. They are your house's <u>circulatory system</u>.

collision—*n.* the slamming of one thing into another. When there is a <u>collision</u> between an opponent's bat and my best pitch, that is not good.

combustible—*adj.* flammable. My science teacher tells us when a material we are working on is especially <u>combustible</u>. When we are working with <u>combustible</u> materials, all Bunsen burners are turned off!

complement—*v.* to make complete. In science, the word is often used to describe how an organ's structure <u>complements</u> its function. The shape of your esophagus (throat) <u>complements</u> its function by being straight and slippery—so food slides down it easily.

complex—*adj.* complicated; not simple. There is almost nothing about science that isn't incredibly <u>complex</u>. The Earth, the universe, your body, the birth of a flea: all of these things are very, very <u>complex</u>.

component—*n.* a part of a system or machine. The <u>components</u> of my stereo are the receiver, the CD player, and the five-speaker surround sound system.

compost—*n.* decayed organic matter that is used as fertilizer. <u>Compost</u> is made of a mixture of dead plants, and maybe manure. It smells awful, but it makes my mom's tomatoes grow fast.

condensation point—*n.* the temperature at which a gas condenses into a liquid. Clouds formed over the Dodgers' last home game when the air temperature reached the <u>condensation point</u>. Clouds form when liquid collects on dust particles in the air.

conductor—*n.* a material that takes an electric current from one point to another. Copper wire is a good <u>conductor</u>. So are you, so stay away from electricity!

conservation—*n.* the protection of natural resources. <u>Conservation</u> is important if we are to keep the few natural wonders this country has left, like the Grand Canyon and Yellowstone National Park.

consistency—*n.* the degree of firmness or viscosity of a substance. A tub of margarine has a <u>consistency</u> similar to soft ice cream. The <u>consistency</u> of motor oil depends on the temperature—it gets really thick and gooey as the temperature drops.

contaminate—*v.* to make impure. Lots of things we do every day <u>contaminate</u> the environment. Driving a car <u>contaminates</u> the environment with carbon monoxide and other gases. Eating fast food <u>contaminates</u> the environment with all of the packaging it comes in, not to mention the pollution from the factories that make the packaging. It's almost like if you don't live in an underground house fueled by solar panels and windmills, you are <u>contaminating</u> the environment! About all we can do is try to reduce the amount of <u>contaminants</u> we produce, but we can never eliminate them.

continental drift—*n.* the theory that the continents are always drifting—they are not fixed. The continents drift only an inch or so each year, but over millions of years, those inches turn into miles.

Think of a train conductor getting you from one point to the next.

DOUBLE MEANING

consistency—n. the ability to be counted on to behave the same way or produce the same thing all the time.

continuity—*n.* uninterrupted succession. One of the things that has helped the Yankees dominate baseball for the last five years is the <u>continuity</u> on the team from year to year. There are always some changes, but the best players and the manager have remained the same.

cumulative—*adj.* the adding of things over time. The <u>cumulative</u> effects of age have caused my parents to become forgetful and slow.

cyclical—*adj.* happening in cycles. In chemistry, the word <u>cyclical</u> has to do with chemical compounds that have atoms arranged in a closed chain. In real life, lots of things are <u>cyclical</u>. The changing of seasons is the most obvious.

cytoplasm—*n.* the protoplasm outside the cell's nucleus.

decay—*v.* to rot; to break down. When you die, unless you have yourself cryogenically frozen or you are cremated, your body will <u>decay</u>. I plan on going the cryogenically frozen route, like in the original *Austin Powers* movie. Groovy baby, yeah!

decompose—*v.* to rot; to break down. See *decay* above.

dehydrate—*v.* to remove the water from. <u>Dehydrated</u> food like beef jerky has had the water taken out—that's why it's all shriveled. A few games ago I got <u>dehydrated</u> and started feeling dizzy because I didn't drink enough water and it was 98 degrees out.

density—*n.* the mass of an object divided by its volume. Metal is more dense than wood. Fudge is more <u>dense</u> than whipped cream. Just remember, light things are usually less <u>dense</u> than heavy things.

deplete—*v.* to use up. One of the main problems today is the gradual <u>depletion</u> of Earth's resources.

deteriorate—*v.* to get worse. When you hear someone say "his health is <u>deteriorating</u>," that means it is getting worse. When you hear someone say "that house is <u>deteriorating</u>" that means it is falling apart because no one is keeping it up.

digestive system—*n.* the parts of your body that work together to break down food so it can be converted into energy. Your <u>digestive system</u> is made up of the alimentary canal, which is basically every part of your body the food touches, from your mouth all the way down to . . . well, you know.

dissolve—*v.* to mix with a liquid. Kool Aid <u>dissolves</u> in water to make a tasty, refreshing drink.

distill—*v.* to purify by evaporation and then condensation. <u>Distilled</u> water has had all of the impurities boiled out. What they do is boil the water and then capture the steam—that steam doesn't have any of the impurities that were in the water. They then drop the temperature on the steam and—ta da!—<u>distilled</u> water.

dominant trait—*n.* when paired with a recessive trait, this is the trait that "wins"—the <u>dominant</u> trait beats the recessive trait. So if the <u>dominant</u> trait in a species of butterfly is big wings and the recessive trait is little wings, a butterfly that has one gene for each will have big wings.

dormant—*adj.* sleeping; inactive. Lots of animals, insects, and

WhizTip
Whenever you see a word with "plasm" in it, you know it has something to do with cells.

WhizTip
I have found that when I don't read regularly, my vocabulary starts to deteriorate.

plants go <u>dormant</u> over the winter, sleeping until spring. When the Dodgers' bats go <u>dormant</u>, that means no one is getting any hits, and the team is doomed.

dynamic—*adj.* related to energy and motion. The Lakers have been a more <u>dynamic</u> team since Kobe and Shaq started playing nice with each other. There is more motion in the offense, and both of them seem to get four or five monster dunks a game.

eclipse—*v.* to block the light. When the moon <u>eclipses</u> the sun, it's always a big deal. It's all over the news, people are making special <u>eclipse</u> viewers out of paper and cardboard boxes. It's bigger than Groundhog Day! As you have probably heard a million times, never look at an <u>eclipse</u>. It could make you go blind.

ecosystem—*n.* the combination of organisms and the place they live. My backyard is an <u>ecosystem</u> all by itself. It's got my dad's Koi pond filled with goldfish and frogs, my mom's lemon trees, and all of the bugs and other animals that call my backyard home. There are probably hundreds of species of plants and animals making up the <u>ecosystem</u> back there.

efficient—*adj.* not wasting time or energy. I have often found that I study most <u>efficiently</u> when there is no noise. If I turn on the radio or TV, it takes me forever to get anything done.

electron—*n.* a tiny particle in an atom's nucleus that has a negative charge. There are the same number of protons (+) and <u>electrons</u> (–) in an atom's nucleus. Their opposite charges cancel each other out.

element—*n.* a substance that has only one kind of atom. There are 118-or-so <u>elements</u>. My favorite is helium, because it's the <u>element</u> that makes your voice high and squeaky.

endocrine system—*n.* the body's endocrine glands, ductless organs that secrete hormones directly into the blood. The <u>endocrine system</u> includes the thyroid, pituitary, and adrenal glands, plus a bunch more I don't have room to list here. (See "The Body" exercise for all of its components.)

endothermic—*adj.* absorbing heat. Think of <u>indoors</u> for <u>endothermic</u> reactions. It's a reaction that brings heat "inside."

entropy—*n.* disorder or chaos in a system. So if the Dodgers have three injured players, they have <u>entropy</u> on the team—disorder and chaos.

epicenter—*n.* the location directly over the center of an earthquake. You hear the word on the nightly news all the time when they are talking about earthquakes, like "The <u>epicenter</u> of the earthquake is located 150 miles west of San Diego, right here where I am standing! Aaaaaaahhhgggghhh!" And then the camera fritzes off.

equilibrium—*n.* a condition in which all forces cancel each other out, resulting in balance. Remember it by thinking of the word "equal." <u>Equilibrium</u> happens when opposing forces are <u>equal</u>.

erosion—*n.* the process of soil being worn away, usually by water and wind. A huge windstorm in Southern California caused a lot of <u>erosion</u>—a bunch of topsoil was basically blown over to New Mexico.

Name five organisms that are part of an ecosystem at or near your home.

1. _____
2. _____
3. _____
4. _____
5. _____

exothermic—**adj.** releasing heat. Think of an EXIT sign for exothermic reactions.

eruption—*n*. the explosion of a volcano. The <u>eruption</u> of Mount Vesuvius in A.D. 79 ended up burying two entire cities in lava and ash. They have only recently started excavating the site.

evaporation—*n*. the process of a liquid turning into a gas. I left a glass of Kool Aid on my bedroom windowsill and forgot about it. A few weeks later, all the liquid had <u>evaporated</u>, and all that was left was red, crusty goo. (Also see the definitions in this section for *distill* and *condensation point*.)

evolve—*v*. to change for the better. The theory of evolution is based on the idea that animals <u>evolve</u> to better take advantage of their environment. So if the environment is full of scary, spike-headed monsters, it would be good for a species to <u>evolve</u> in ways that would protect it from the monsters. (Thick skins and fast legs come to mind.)

exothermic—*adj*. releasing heat. An <u>exothermic</u> reaction happens when substances react strongly to each other. For example, if you mix two substances in a test tube and the tube gets hot, that's an <u>exothermic</u> reaction. Heat has been released. (See *endothermic* for more on this.)

extinct—*adj*. no longer in existence. The dodo bird is <u>extinct</u>—there aren't any of them on the planet any more. Dinosaurs are <u>extinct</u>. My mom says real gentlemen are <u>extinct</u>. (I'm not sure what that means.)

extrapolate—*v*. to take things you know and make assumptions based on those things. If you have gotten As on all your science tests so far, you can <u>extrapolate</u> that you will get good grades on the rest of your science tests, too.

extraterrestrial—*adj*. outside the Earth. Lots of people think there are <u>extraterrestrial</u> beings in outer space. I think they're nuts.

fault—*n*. a break in a rock formation. Earthquakes happen along geologic <u>faults</u>, where a rock formation is broken and two big slabs of rock are rubbing against each other.

fissure—*n*. a crack in a rock. Earthquakes usually form along <u>fissures</u>, where the rock is rubbing against itself.

food chain—*n*. a line of organisms that eat each other.

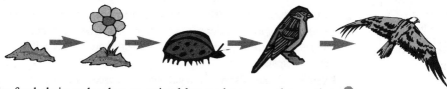

The <u>food chain</u> ends when an animal has no known predator—that means no other animals eat it. (Most hawks have nothing to fear.)

fossil fuel—*n*. fuel made from decayed organisms. Coal and oil are actually dead plants and animals that have decayed and have been compressed over millions of years into <u>fossil fuels</u>. Wind is not a <u>fossil fuel</u>. Neither is solar energy. They are renewable resources. (See the definition for *renewable*.)

friction—*n*. rough rubbing. The <u>friction</u> between rock formations is what causes earthquakes. (See *fissure*.)

Whiz Quiz

Do an Internet search and find the most recent volcano eruption in the United States.

Whiz Quiz

Name three more extinct animals or species:

1. _____
2. _____
3. _____

Science

fusion—*n.* in physics, a reaction in which atoms join together. In chemistry, when two substances are melted and mixed together. Basically, <u>fusion</u> takes place when two separate things combine into one thing.

galaxy—*n.* a big group of stars. The Earth and the sun and all of our sun's other planets are part of the Milky Way <u>galaxy</u>.

gene—*n.* a section of a chromosome that controls how part of an organism turns out. You have <u>genes</u> that control your eye color, your height, your looks—everything. And we are learning more and more about <u>genes</u> every day. Scientists just completed charting every <u>gene</u>—it was called the Human Genome Project.

generation—*n.* a group of people born around the same time; a stage in a succession. I have heard people calling our <u>generation</u> "Generation I" because we are the first to grow up with computers and the Internet.

genetics—*n.* the study of genes and heredity. The field of <u>genetics</u> is really booming right now. All of the stuff they are finding out about genes and how they affect our health and everything about us is really cool. Some people even think <u>genetics</u> will be the key to curing cancer!

greenhouse effect—*n.* the result of too many pollutants in the atmosphere; they let the sunlight in, but they don't let the heat back out. That causes the atmosphere to act like a greenhouse—keeping the heat in. Some people think the <u>greenhouse effect</u> is causing all the glaciers to melt around the polar icecaps.

groundwater—*n.* the water underneath the soil. Lots of people are afraid things like garbage dumps, strip mines, and nuclear waste sites are polluting the <u>groundwater</u>.

habitat—*n.* the normal environment where an organism lives. A water turtle's natural <u>habitat</u> is a pond. A hermit crab's natural <u>habitat</u> is the ocean. That's why, when we have them as pets, we try to re-create their <u>habitat</u> inside an aquarium with rocks, sand, water, and some driftwood to climb on.

hemisphere—*n.* in earth sciences, the northern or southern half of the Earth. The equator is what separates the northern and southern <u>hemispheres</u>. To remember it, think <u>hemisphere</u> = half-a-sphere.

herbivore—*n.* an animal that eats plants. Cows are <u>herbivores</u>. Horses are <u>herbivores</u>. Vegetarians are <u>herbivores</u>. They all eat veggies, no meats.

hybrid—*n.* the offspring you get when you breed two different kinds of parents. You most often hear the word <u>hybrid</u> when people are talking about plants, like a corn <u>hybrid</u> that fends off insects or a <u>hybrid</u> tomato that is bigger and juicier than any other kind of tomato ever.

hydroelectric—*adj.* relating to electricity generated by water turning a turbine. My aunt in New York works at a public radio station that is run on <u>hydroelectric</u> power! All their power comes from a dam in a river outside the station.

hypothesis—*n.* a proposed explanation. Scientific progress is based on proving or disproving a <u>hypothesis</u>. If your <u>hypothesis</u> is

To remember galaxy, think of the first *Star Wars* movie that starts out with the words "In a galaxy far far away . . . ."

Think of a name for your generation that is better than Generation I.

The United Nations did an environmental study that concluded that the greenhouse effect is going to raise the average temperature of the Earth two to four degrees in the next 100 years.

DOUBLE MEANING

hemisphere—n. also stands for one-half of the brain—the left and right hemispheres.

There is a big debate about what to do with the dams in the West that produce hydroelectric power. Some want to destroy them and restore the rivers—and the fish.

64

"plants are mean," and you do an experiment that proves plants are mean, then your hypothesis is correct. If the experiment does not prove plants are mean, that DOES NOT mean the <u>hypothesis</u> is incorrect, only that your experiment didn't prove it.

igneous rock—*n.* rock that is formed from molten lava. It's not metamorphic, it's not sedimentary—it's <u>igneous</u>! (See the definition for *rock cycle*.)

ignite—*v.* to light on fire. When you <u>ignite</u> your Bunsen burner in science class, it gives off a blue flame.

immune—*adj.* being resistant to something bad. Lots of time you hear this word when people are talking about AIDS. AIDS is an acronym for Acquired Immunodeficiency Syndrome. It's a disease that attacks your <u>immune</u> system, and makes it so you can't fight off any bacteria or other bad germs.

incinerate—*v.* to burn until there is nothing left but ashes. If you flew a space shuttle toward the sun, the sun's heat would <u>incinerate</u> it.

inertia—*n.* resistance to motion. My dad has a lot of <u>inertia</u> on weekends. It's hard to get him off the couch.

insulation—*n.* protective material. There are lots of different kinds of <u>insulation</u> in your house. Heat <u>insulation</u> keeps heat from escaping your house. Water pipe <u>insulation</u> keeps them from freezing when it's cold. There is also <u>insulation</u> around electrical wires that keeps the wires from shocking everything they touch!

interact—*v.* to be involved with something else. Science is always testing how different things <u>interact</u>. It can be chemicals that <u>interact</u> with each other in an experiment; it can be animals <u>interacting</u> with each other in a habitat; it can be how the orbits of planets <u>interact</u> with each other.

interdependent—*adj.* relating to two things that rely on each other; mutual dependence. All habitats and ecosystems survive because the organisms in them are <u>interdependent</u>. One example of <u>interdependence</u> is flowers needing bees for pollination and bees needing flowers for their nectar.

intestine—*n.* one of two long tubes in your gut where food is digested. The small <u>intestine</u> measures about 22 feet long, and the large <u>intestine</u> measures about five feet long.

ion—*n.* an atom or molecule that used to be electrically neutral, but now it is either positive or negative because it gained or lost electrons. In other words, it used to be neutral (same number of protons and electrons) but it has since gained or lost an electron, so it is a positive <u>ion</u> (lost electrons) or negative <u>ion</u> (gained electrons).

kinetic—*adj.* having to do with movement. Most often, it is used to describe <u>kinetic</u> energy. To remember <u>kinetic</u>, think of calisthenics. They kind of sound the same, and they both have to do with movement.

lethal—*adj.* causing death. Some states with capital punishment, like Texas, use a <u>lethal</u> injection to kill the prisoners on death row.

light year—*n.* the distance light travels in one year (9.46×10^{12} kilo-

Identify the rock's type:

basalt

granite

limestone

marble

What's another kind of insulation? Try to think of one.

Which is longer?

100 feet of string or your small intestine

2,000 miles of highway or your small intestine

350-meter running track or your small intestine

Six yards of fabric or your small intestine

List three things that are lethal to humans:

1.
2.
3.

meters). It's important to remember that a <u>light year</u> is a measure of distance, not time.

lithosphere—*n.* the Earth's crust. All of the valleys, mountains, plains, and meadows, plus all of the bottoms of the seas, rivers, and lakes, make up the <u>lithosphere</u>.

lunar—*adj.* having to do with the moon. A <u>lunar</u> eclipse is when the Earth blocks the sun's light to the moon. The <u>lunar</u> module is a space-ship that landed on the moon.

magma—*n.* the molten rock below the Earth's surface, waiting to spew out in a volcano and then form igneous rock when it cools. I went on a vacation to Hawaii and I actually saw red, glowing <u>magma</u> where there are active volcanoes.

magnitude—*n.* a measure of the amount of energy an earthquake releases. Earthquakes' <u>magnitudes</u> are always measured. Small earthquakes have <u>magnitudes</u> from 2–3. Medium-size earthquakes have <u>magnitudes</u> from 4–6. Large earthquakes have <u>magnitudes</u> from 7–10.

mantle—*n.* the layer of rock between the Earth's crust and its core. So, we walk all over the crust, the core is boiling molten rock, and the only thing keeping the molten rock from us crust-dwellers is the <u>mantle</u>. Thank you, <u>mantle</u>!

meiosis—*n.* cell division in sexually reproducing organisms that produces a cell with half the required number of chromosomes that will then link up with the other half of the chromosomes from the other sex partner. Humans have 46 chromosomes—23 from each parent. <u>Meiosis</u> is what produces one of those 23-chromosome sex cells (called gametes).

membrane—*n.* as in cell membrane, the outer layer of the cell. The <u>membrane</u> keeps all the stuff inside the cell from floating out AND it keeps out the stuff the cell doesn't need.

metabolism—*n.* the chemical and physical changes that take place in cells; the changes that take place in the body. You have probably heard people say "I have a high <u>metabolism</u>—I eat anything I want all day and I don't gain a pound." Someone with a high <u>metabolism</u> has a body that is working really fast and efficiently to burn up all the food it gets.

metamorphic rock—*n.* rock that was changed from one kind of rock to another by pressure or temperature. It's not sedimentary, it's not igneous—it's <u>metamorphic</u>! (See the definition for *rock cycle*.)

meteor—*n.* the trail behind a meteorite caused by the meteorite entering the Earth's atmosphere. Last year I saw the most awesome <u>meteor</u> shower I have ever seen. It was like the sky was on fire—there were so many <u>meteors</u> burning up as they entered

Related Word

metamorphosis—n. the change from one thing to another.

Related Word

meteorite—n. a space rock that enters the Earth's atmosphere and makes a meteor.

our atmosphere.

mineral—*n.* a natural substance with a definite chemical and crystalline composition. A diamond is a <u>mineral</u>. So are gold and silver.

mitochondrion—*n.* the part of the cell that converts food into energy. It's at the last stage of digestion, working to turn that burger and fries into energy for your body.

mitosis—*n.* the division of a cell into two identical cells; the differentiation and segregation of replicated chromosomes in a cell's nucleus.

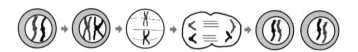

molecule—*n.* the smallest unit of a compound or an element. A <u>molecule</u> of water has two hydrogen and one oxygen atom—H_2O.

molten—*adj.* melted or liquefied by intense heat. The lava that comes out of volcanoes is <u>molten</u> rock.

mutation—*n.* a change in the genes of an organism from one generation to the next. The theory of evolution states that a <u>mutation</u> that helps an organism survive better than others will be passed down from generation to generation, because that organism and its offspring will have a better chance of living and having kids. That's why giraffes have long necks. They lived in a place where the food was up high, so the ones with the genetic <u>mutation</u> that gave them longer necks did better and had more kids than the ones with shorter necks, who couldn't get to the food, and died.

natural selection—*n.* the theory that organisms best suited for their environment survive and have offspring, and those who are not die and do not have offspring. Also known as "survival of the fittest." Kind of harsh, I know. But it is the way things work in nature. (See *mutation* for more on this.)

neutron—*n.* a particle that's in the nucleus of all atoms (except hydrogen). A <u>neutron</u> has the same mass as a proton, but no electrical charge (it is neutral). So the nucleus of atoms has protons, electrons, and <u>neutrons</u> (except hydrogen).

nuclear energy—*n.* the energy released by a nuclear reaction. <u>Nuclear energy</u> makes up a big part of this country's energy production, but not near as much as energy produced by burning oil, coal, and natural gas. The thing is, <u>nuclear energy</u> plants can be much more dangerous than other energy sources. If something goes wrong and radiation escapes from a <u>nuclear power</u> plant, people can get sick and die.

nucleus—*n.* 1) the center of a cell containing the genes. The <u>nucleus</u> of a cell contains the parts that control the cell, like the <u>nucleus</u> of a baseball team is made up of the players that control whether a team wins or loses. 2) In an atom, the center of the atom containing protons, electrons, and neutrons.

nutrients—*n.* the stuff that nourishes your body. You see the word all the time on vitamin commercials—"VitaMight contains 127 essential <u>nutrients</u> to keep your body glowing like a lightbulb!" The fact is you get plenty of <u>nutrients</u> from the foods you eat, as long as you eat the right foods.

omnivore—*n.* an organism that eats all kinds of food, including plants and animals. Humans are <u>omnivores</u>. So are dogs.

orbit—*n.* the path of one celestial body around another. Planets occupy different <u>orbits</u> around the sun.

organic—*adj.* having to do with living organisms. When you see food labeled "organic" in the grocery store, that means it was grown with all <u>organic</u> materials—no chemicals or man-made substances were used.

organism—*n.* a living plant, animal, bacterium, protist, or fungus. I have used the word <u>organism</u> in tons of these science definitions. It's obviously because lots of science is concerned with the study of <u>organisms</u> and all of the things that affect <u>organisms</u>.

oxidation—*n.* a reaction in which the atoms in an element lose electrons. The most common example of <u>oxidation</u> is the formation of rust. Metal atoms <u>oxidize</u>—they lose electrons—and rust forms.

ozone layer—*n.* a layer of our atmosphere that protects us from harmful sun rays. Pollution is causing holes in the <u>ozone layer</u>, which means those bad sun rays are making it all the way down to the Earth, where they can cause skin cancer. My mom always makes me wear sunscreen when I go surfing because she's worried about the holes in the <u>ozone layer</u>.

periodic table—*n.* the chart that lists all of the elements and their atomic numbers.

5	6	7	8
B	C	N	O
13	14	15	16
Al	Si	P	S
31	32	33	34
Ga	Ge	As	Se

pH—*n.* a measure of how acidic or alkaline a substance is.

photosynthesis—*n.* the process plants use to turn sunlight into energy. If people could perform <u>photosynthesis</u>, we wouldn't need to eat so much! We could just sit in the sun and get all the energy we need. Instead we have to cover ourselves in sunscreen and stay in the shade. Lucky plants!

precipitation—*n.* rain, snow, sleet, and hail. The weatherman said the odds of <u>precipitation</u> tomorrow are 50 percent. But he's never right.

Related Word

**predatory—adj.
like a hunter.**

predator—*n.* an animal that hunts another. A shark is a fierce <u>predator</u>, hunting other fish continuously, never sleeping, always hungry.

protein—*n.* a compound in all living things that helps organisms grow and repair themselves. Good sources of <u>protein</u> are beef and beans and eggs—which all happen to be in my favorite omelet!

proton—*n.* a positively charged particle in an atom. (See definitions of *electron* and *neutron*.)

protoplasm—*n.* a jellylike substance that forms all the living matter in plants and animals. That's right, the basis for all living things is a jiggly mass of jelly. Kind of gross when you think about it, so I try not to.

protozoa—*n.* primitive, single-celled organisms. <u>Protozoa</u> might be what the earliest forms of life on Earth were like.

pulley—*n.* a wheel with a groove in it that a rope fits on. By using <u>pulleys</u>, you can lift really, really heavy things. I went to a museum where a rope was attached to a 2,000-pound weight. It went through a series of <u>pulleys</u> so you could lift 2,000 pounds with one hand. It was wild.

radiation—*n.* the emission of waves or particles. Nuclear <u>radiation</u> is waves and particles given off by radioactive material. It can be really dangerous and even lethal.

recessive trait—*n.* when paired with a dominant trait, it is the trait that "loses." (See the definition for *dominant trait*.)

refraction—*n.* the deflection of a particle wave, usually a light or sound wave. *Example*: When light passes through water, it bends.

regulate—*v.* to control. Our brain is our body's main <u>regulator</u>. It controls breathing, heartbeat, appetite—you name it, the brain probably <u>regulates</u> it.

renewable—*adj.* able to be used again. Most often used in the term "<u>renewable</u> resources" to describe sources of energy that can be used again and again. Two examples are wind and sunlight—they are forms of energy that you can use over and over without using them up.

reproduction—*n.* the process by which living things produce offspring. Most animals and plants use sexual <u>reproduction</u>, where the offspring gets half its chromosomes from each parent. In asexual <u>reproduction</u>, the offspring gets all its genetic material from one parent. The formation of spores is a good example of asexual <u>reproduction</u>.

resistant—*adj.* able to fight off something. Some crops are engineered to be <u>resistant</u> to certain bugs. Some bacteria become <u>resistant</u> to drugs that are used to kill them. So <u>resistance</u> can be good for us (crops that can fend off pests) and bad for us (diseases that are <u>resistant</u> to treatment).

respiratory system—*n.* the group of organs that keep you breathing. If you think of it in terms of your house, things that circulate air—like fans and air conditioners—are your house's <u>respiratory</u> system. (See "The Body" exercise for all of the organs involved in Britney Spears' <u>respiratory system</u>.)

revolve—*v.* to move in a circular motion around a center. The Earth <u>revolves</u> around the sun. The Lakers <u>revolve</u> around Shaq. You get the picture.

rock cycle—*n.* a rock's "life cycle," in which a rock goes from

Whiz Fact

The Incredible Hulk was created when scientist Bruce Banner was accidentally exposed to radiation.

igneous to sedimentary to metamorphic by going through erosion, crushing, pressure, melting, and everything else rocks go through.

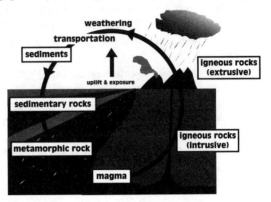

rotate—*n.* to turn on an axis. The Earth rotates on its axis. So do the other planets.

satellite—*n.* a man-made object shot into space that orbits the Earth or another planet. Most <u>satellites</u> these days are used for communication, but there are also science <u>satellites</u> and military <u>satellites.</u>

scientific method—*n.* the process of observing something, forming a hypothesis for how it works, doing experiments to test that hypothesis, and then drawing conclusions from your results. So, if from watching bears at the San Diego Zoo, you form the hypothesis that bears are dumb as rocks, you do an experiment to test them. Maybe you ask them their names. When they don't know the answer, you conclude your hypothesis is correct—they don't know their names, they must be dumb as rocks. (You can see why the <u>scientific method</u> isn't perfect!)

sedimentary rock—*n.* rock that is formed near the Earth's surface by the accumulation of sediment. It's not metamorphic, it's not igneous—it's <u>sedimentary</u>! (See the definition for *rock cycle*.)

selective breeding—*n.* the process of choosing which plants or animals to breed with each other. You do this when you are looking to promote a particular trait. So if you are breeding poodles and you want poodles with extra long ears, you <u>selectively breed</u> the long-eared poodles. (You give the short-eared poodles away to friends.)

solar—*adj.* having to do with the sun. The <u>solar</u> system is the system of planets revolving around the sun. <u>Solar</u> flares are eruptions that spew from the sun and mess up our television reception. <u>Solar</u>caine stops sunburn pain when someone you love is hurting.

soluble—*adj.* dissolvable. Sugar is <u>soluble</u> in water. So is Kool Aid.

solvent—*n.* a liquid that dissolves another substance. Water is a <u>solvent</u> for many substances, including sugar, salt, and Kool Aid.

stimulus—*n.* something that causes a response. An organism is always responding to both internal and external <u>stimuli</u>. For example, a toad responds to external <u>stimuli</u> like predators and temperature and internal <u>stimuli</u> like hunger and the urge to reproduce.

The first satellite was launched by the Russians in 1957. It was called Sputnik.

Remember, soluble things can be dissolved.

sustainable—*adj.* able to maintain over a period of time. One of the ways to fight world hunger is to find <u>sustainable</u> crops that starving countries can grow themselves. There is a Chinese proverb: "Give a man a fish and he will eat for a day. Teach a man to fish and he will eat for the rest of his life." That's the idea behind teaching people in these countries to grow <u>sustainable</u> crops.

tarnish—*v.* to dull the luster of. *Example*: Brass beds tarnish when they are exposed to air and the oils on your hands.

tectonic plates—*n.* the huge plates that make up the continents and the floors of the oceans. They shift a little all of the time. The friction where the <u>tectonic plates</u> meet causes scary stuff to happen, including earthquakes, mountain formation, and tidal waves.

temperate—*adj.* not hot, not cold. This word is most often used when talking about <u>temperate</u> climates, where animals and plants thrive because the temperature does not get too hot or cold.

topography—*n.* the physical features of a place. A region's <u>topography</u> can include mountains, plains, lakes, rivers, oceans, and every other kind of geographical feature.

toxic—*adj.* harmful; dangerous. Scientists deal with <u>toxic</u> materials all of the time. Sometimes we even work with them in science class ourselves. Stuff like mercury and dry ice is pretty cool, but they can be very <u>toxic</u>, so be careful.

trait—*n.* a characteristic; a feature. I share a lot of physical <u>traits</u> with my dad—we both have brown eyes, high foreheads, and winning smiles.

transform—*v.* to change from one thing into another. Coal <u>transforms</u> into diamonds under intense pressure after millions of years.

vacuum—*n.* a space where there is no matter. Lots of science experiments have to be done in a <u>vacuum</u> to work. For example, in a <u>vacuum</u>, a feather and a brick fall at the same rate, because there is no matter—air—to make the feather float more slowly.

vapor—*n.* stuff that looks like mist, fumes, or smoke. Steam is the <u>vapor</u> form of water.

velocity—*n.* speed. The highest <u>velocity</u> I have ever thrown my fastball is 72 mph.

vital—*adj.* pertaining to life; important. A person's <u>vital</u> signs are the measurements of the things keeping him alive, like heart rate, blood pressure, and brain activity.

watt—*n.* the fleshy orange fold of skin under a turkey's neck. Wait—that's a wattle! A <u>watt</u> is a unit of electricity. If you want to save electricity, change all the light bulbs in your house to 40-<u>watt</u> or 60-<u>watt</u> bulbs.

WhizQuiz

What kinds of sustainable crops are produced in your part of the state?

WhizTip

Think of Goldilocks: not too hot and not too cold, the "temperate porridge" is just right!

WhizQuiz

Nature is full of transformations. Name three:
1. _____
2. _____
3. _____

71

Exercises

WhizWords

acclimatization
conservation
ecosystem
fossil fuel
greenhouse effect
habitat
organism

Science
The Environment

Have you ever heard of Woody Guthrie? He was a folk singer who wrote hundreds of songs about America. He would travel the country hitchhiking and riding on freight trains, getting to know the people he met along the way. He ended up writing classics like "This Land Is Your Land," "Pastures of Plenty," and "Do-Re-Mi." (No, not the song about "a female deer" and "a drop of golden sun." A different "Do-Re-Mi.")

Guthrie was also a big environmentalist. He was really alarmed by all of the factories he saw going up around the country. He saw America as an expanse of forests and plains and deserts and lakes and rivers. And he saw it changing into an expanse of roads and cities and houses and, well, people.

My dad loves Woody Guthrie. He is always humming "This Land Is Your Land" and putting in his own words. So when he has to cut the grass, he likes to sing, "This land is your land, this land is my land, I've got to cut the grass, that'll keep me smilin'." It can get annoying, but it gave me a great idea for how to remember environment words.

WRITE A FOLK SONG EXERCISE

What I want you to do is use each of these "Environment" words in a verse of "This Land Is Your Land." You want to squish the word and the definition into the verse. It may not win you any Grammys, but if you spend some time on it and fit all seven words into seven verses, you'll have a little hummable song about the environment. And you can hum it during a test if you need to remember the words!

I'll get you started with a verse about one of the WhizWords above—
fossil fuel.

♫ **This land is your land,**
this land is my land,
Fossil fuel emits carbon monoxide,
when you burn it in your car, man. ♫

If you have another song you want to use instead of "This Land Is Your Land," by all means, go ahead. If you've never even heard "This Land Is Your Land," ask your music teacher to hum a few bars, or go on the Internet to *www.geocities.com/Nashville/3448/thisl1.html* to hear a snippet.

Science

The Body

By the end of middle school you should have a pretty good idea of what the different parts of the body do. The four main systems of the body aren't that hard to understand, but there are a lot of organs in each one, so it's good to be able to organize the organs by the systems they are in.

Just remember: the **circulatory system** has to do with circulating the blood. The **digestive system** has to do with organs that help you digest your food. The **respiratory system** does your breathing for you (to remember the word, think about being put on a respirator—a machine that breathes for you). And the **endocrine system**, well, it helps get the bad stuff out of your blood. Crime is bad—so think about the endo*crime* system getting the bad stuff out of your blood. Close enough!

LABELING YOUR INNARDS EXERCISE
I have listed the major organs in each system. Your challenge is to label them in this Britney Spears body outline. Check the answer key when you are done.

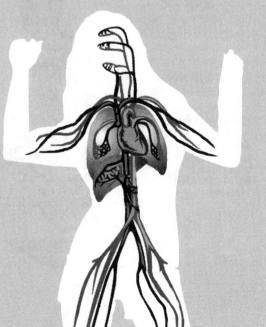

Circulatory System
arteries
capillaries
heart
lungs
veins

Science

Digestive System →
anus
esophagus
large intestine
mouth
small intestine
stomach

Respiratory System →
diaphragm
lungs
nose
pharynx (throat)
ribcage
trachea

The Body

Endocrine System →
adrenal gland
hypothalamus
ovaries (female)
pancreas
pituitary gland
testes (male)
thyroid gland

Exercises

WhizWords

asteroids
eclipse
extraterrestrial
galaxy
light year
lunar
meteor
orbit
ozone layer
satellite
solar

Related Word

celestial—adj.
Asteroids and
satellites are
both celestial
bodies, as they
are part of the
universe.

Science
The Universe

Sometimes I just lie on my back in my backyard at night and look up at the sky and imagine what the astronauts on the International Space Station must think when they look out the window. Have you ever seen the movie *Apollo 13* or spent any time on NASA's website? The pictures of space from the windows of spacecraft are just incredible.

And now it looks like normal citizens are going to be able to go into space, just like the astronauts. In 2001, an American businessman named Dennis Tito became the first space tourist when he paid $20 million to join a Russian space crew on a trip to the International Space Station. So someday, you may get to travel in space, whether you're an astronaut or not.

DRAWING THE UNIVERSE EXERCISE

For this exercise you get to draw and label the universe, from the perspective of an astronaut on the old Mir. I have provided the Earth, its moon, and the sun. You can draw and/or label the rest of the "Universe" words above. For example:

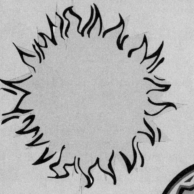

LABEL OR DRAW
distance to sun in light years
a partial eclipse
the moon's orbit
the Earth's ozone layer
a satellite

76

WhizWords

cell
dominant trait
gene
genetics
recessive trait
trait

Science

Genetics

My friend Gene has curly red hair and freckles just like his father and all of his brothers. That's how I remember that a **gene** is the part of the **cell** that decides which **traits** will be passed from one generation to the next.

But sometimes **genetics** don't work out quite so logically. For instance, my sister Aimee is really tall: 5'9". Both of my parents are short. So am I. So what happened to Aimee? There must have been a **recessive** "tall" **gene** that both of my parents carried that, against the odds, made it into my sister. The same goes for her eye color. My parents both have brown eyes. I have brown eyes. My sister has blue eyes. So what happened to Aimee? Again, a **recessive trait** in both my parents ended up being expressed in my freaky sister. Here's how that happens:

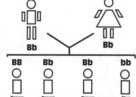

See *Innerspace!*
It's a movie that
came out in 1987
about a Navy
pilot who gets
miniaturized
and injected into
the body of a
hypochondriac.

As you can see, the odds are greater that my parents would have would have children with brown eyes, because that is the **dominant gene** for eye color. All you need is one brown eyes **gene** to have brown eyes. Aimee just got lucky and was the one kid who got a **recessive** "blue eyes" **gene** from each of my parents.

MOVIE AND TV STAR RECESSIVE TRAITS EXERCISE

Pick out two movie stars. I am going to pick Cher and Billy Crystal. Now, pick a trait. I am going to pick foot size and make big feet dominant and little feet recessive. Draw a chart like the one I drew above, giving each either two dominant genes (FF), two recessives (ff), or one of each (Ff). See how their children would turn out. Here is my Billy + Cher drawing.

In this scenario, it is equally likely that Billy + Cher's child would have big Cher feet (Ff and Ff) or little Billy feet (ff and ff). I don't even want to think about what the rest of their bodies would look like.

77

WhizWords

continental drift
erosion
fault
mantle
tectonic plates

Science

Geology

WhizTip

Want to learn about California's earthquakes? Start by going to *pasadena.wr.usgs. gov.*

Living in California, you cannot forget that the world is a big mass of sliding **tectonic plates** drifting toward and away from each other, wreaking havoc where they butt up against each other. Anyone else who has studied the history of the Earth—especially anyone who lives in California—knows that beneath us is a molten core of boiling rock, yearning to break free!

When you think of it this way, geology is pretty cool. In addition to studying the process of **continental drift**, geologists get to hunt for wild-looking fossils and try to piece them together like giant jigsaw puzzles. You can see why there are so many geologists running around, predicting earthquakes and digging up dinosaurs.

EARTHQUAKE EXERCISE

Unfortunately, geology is not always fun and games. Every once in a while a big earthquake hits and people lose their homes and sometimes their lives. The same forces that create mountains also create terrible tragedies.

For this exercise, I want you to research a recent earthquake. There was a massive earthquake in India in 2001 that killed tens of thousands. There was also an earthquake in San Francisco in 1989 that ruined the freeway system and ended up postponing a World Series game that was taking place when it hit!

Once you have compiled some information on an earthquake, turn the page. Write a short essay in the space provided using the words above to explain the tectonic shifts that caused the trembler. Underline the WhizWords in the essay.

Related Word

igneous rock
metamorphic rock
sedimentary rock

Essay

EXPLAIN THE TECTONIC SHIFTS BEHIND A RECENT EARTHQUAKE.

Chapter 5
Test Instructions

Use your pencil when you have reading passages on tests. Underline the topic sentence of each paragraph and circle proper names. It will help slow you down and help you when you refer back to the passage for information.

**Circle your answer to the following best questions:
Which word best describes George W. Bush?**

man woman child

What is your best prediction of how the Dodgers will do this year?

better worse same

Which word best answers the question "Where is Sacramento?"
Earth
California
Not in Minnesota

according to the passage—When you see this phrase, you know the answer to the question is right in the passage you just read. You don't have to use your imagination or remember what you learned in class to find an answer. The answer to the question is in the reading passage.

accurate—*adj.* exactly right. As in "Which of the following is an accurate statement?" This means "Which statement matches the information given?" *Example*: If the information says Aimee spit out her broccoli when her mom wasn't looking because broccoli makes her sick, an accurate statement would be "Aimee can't stand broccoli," not "Aimee can't stand her mother."

approximate—*v.* to come close to; to estimate. Sometimes tests ask you to approximate—that means you are supposed to use the information they give you to make an estimate. Estimates are answers that are close to the real answer. When your car breaks down, the repair shop gives an estimate on how much the repairs will cost. This is approximately how much it will cost. It may be a little more, it may be a little less.

author's purpose—the writer's reason for writing, as in "The author's purpose in this passage is to . . . . " In author's purpose questions, you are looking for what the author was trying to accomplish with his writing. Sometimes an author's purpose is to scare you (horror novel). Sometimes an author's purpose is to convince you to believe something (persuasive article). Think about how you felt after reading the passage—how you felt is probably the author's purpose.

best—*adj.* you'll see this word a lot: "best represents"; "best estimate"; "best prediction"; "best describes"; "the best summary"; "best supported by information in the passage." It means you have to use your "best judgment" and pick the "best answer." You may have a set of answers that may all seem like they could be right, and you have to choose the one that is the best (more right than the others).

complete the pattern—also seen on tests as "if the pattern continues . . . . " This phrase is used on number pattern questions.

WhizList

The test is asking you to find the next number in a number pattern. Figure out what the pattern is, and fill in the next—or missing—number to <u>complete the pattern</u>.

conclude—*v.* to form an opinion based on information. As in "the reader can <u>conclude</u> . . . . " That just means "What did the reader (you) think after reading this passage?"

connotation—*n.* something that suggests more than what has literally been stated or written. For example, in the surfing world, the word "Hawaii" brings with it <u>connotations</u> of tasty waves and the annual surfing nationals.

convince—*v.* to persuade. As in "information to <u>convince</u> the reader . . . . " Some tests ask you if an author provided enough examples to convince you of something. So if I wanted to <u>convince</u> you the Dodgers are going to win the World Series this year, I'd have to provide a ton of reasons to persuade you.

corresponds—*v.* matches; agrees with. Sometimes you are asked to pick the answer that <u>corresponds</u> to the data in the question. That just means it matches. So a test may have a statement like:

The *Star Wars* trilogy became the highest-grossing movie series ever, earning more than $1 billion.

And then it says:

Pick the statement that <u>corresponds</u> to the data given in the statement:

A) The *Star Wars* trilogy lost money.

B) The *Star Wars* trilogy won three Oscars.

C) The *Star Wars* trilogy made a lot of money.

equivalent—*adj.* the same as. Test questions—especially math and science test questions—often want you to find things that are <u>equivalent</u> to one another. That just means finding an answer that is the same as something in the question. So if a test wants you to find the <u>equivalent</u> to a dozen eggs, you pick 12 eggs. If a test wants you to find the <u>equivalent</u> of 1/2 meter, you pick 50 centimeters.

expression—*n.* a way of saying something, usually with a math question. As in "Which <u>expression</u> could be used . . . . " or "Which expression represents . . . . " So you are trying to match the <u>expression</u> to the passage. A passage may say:

Tim bought five eggs, dropped three, and then purchased five more. Which <u>expression</u> represents Tim's egg-buying experience?

A) 5 + 3 + 5

B) 5 − 3 − 5

C) 5 − 3 + 5

fact—*n.* something that actually happened or actually exists. As in "Which of these is a <u>fact</u> from this passage?" When there is a question about <u>facts</u>, there is usually a question about an *opinion*, too. A <u>fact</u> is what actually happened. An *opinion* is what someone thinks happened.

main idea—as in "The <u>main idea</u> of the story." You get a <u>main idea</u> by reading a passage carefully. Sometimes the title of a reading passage offers a clue about the <u>main idea</u>. Sometimes it's better to decide the passage's <u>main idea</u> *before* you read the answer choices. You will usually find your <u>main idea</u> among the answer choices. But if you read the answer choices first, it can get confusing, because usually all the ideas in the answer choices are in the passage, but they aren't the <u>main idea</u>.

method—*n.* one way of doing things. As in "Which <u>method</u> could be used to . . . . " Sometimes math problems ask you which <u>method</u> can be used to get the right answer. This just means "Which of the answer choices is a way you can get the right answer." One way to find out is to do the math problem, and then pick the <u>method</u> you used to get the answer.

most likely—as in "Which is <u>most likely</u> to be true . . . . " This means the answer is what is probably going to happen. At least there is a better chance it will happen than the other answers. The answer to a "<u>most likely</u>" question usually isn't spelled out in the reading passage. You have to guess what is <u>most likely</u> to happen, based on the information in the passage.

opinion—*n.* something someone believes or thinks, whether it is true or not. As in "Which is an <u>opinion</u> in this passage?" Being able to tell the difference between *facts* and *opinions* is important for the reading sections on standardized tests.

probably—*adv.* most likely. Most often used as "<u>probably</u> felt . . . " or "<u>probably</u> believes . . . " or "<u>probably</u> thought . . . . " It just means that the passage doesn't actually state what a character or writer believes, but from reading it, you should be able to tell anyway.

reasonable—*adj.* logical; showing good judgment. <u>Reasonable</u> is like "best." You'll see it all the time: "Which is a <u>reasonable</u> total cost . . . " or "What is a <u>reasonable</u> prediction . . . " or "What is a <u>reasonable</u> conclusion . . . " or "What is a <u>reasonable</u> length . . . . " Who

Circle the facts, underline the opinions:

The Dodgers hit 211 home runs in 2000.

They are going to do better this year.

The Dodgers beat the Athletics when they met in the World Series in 1988.

The Dodgers will beat the Athletics the next time they meet.

WhizTip

Think of the main idea as the "main tent" at a circus. That's where the main show with the elephants and the trapeze artists is. The other parts of the circus are in smaller tents. They are all part of the circus, but the main tent is the main idea. So when you look at the answer choices, think "Is this the elephant in the main tent, or the bearded lady in a smaller tent?"

is the most <u>reasonable</u> person you know? The most <u>reasonable</u> person I can think of is the newsman Tom Brokaw. You know who I'm talking about—he reads the nightly news for one of the networks. He seems very <u>reasonable</u>—like I can trust him. Whenever I get a "reasonable" question, I think—which answer would Mr. <u>Reasonable</u>, Tom Brokaw, choose? You can do the same thing. Just pick out the most <u>reasonable</u> person you know and try to choose the answer you think he would choose.

reason to believe—as in "gives the reader <u>reason to believe</u> . . . ." This means the passage makes you think one way, not the other way. For example, here's a sample passage: "The Raiders have drafted the 10 best players in college football, and the other teams in the NFL weren't allowed to draft anyone at all." This passage gives you <u>reason to believe</u> that:

a) The Raiders will get better.

b) The other teams in the NFL will get better.

The answer is (a). You have <u>reason to believe</u> that if the Raiders got all the good players and the other teams didn't get any players at all, the Raiders will get better, not the other teams, even though it doesn't actually say that in the passage.

rounded to the nearest—as in " . . . <u>rounded to the nearest</u> thousand." When a test question asks you to round off, that means you go to the place given (tens, hundreds, thousands) and round up or down. If the next number is five or higher, you round up one. If the next number is four or lower, you round down one. On "<u>rounded to the nearest</u>" questions, it's very important to pay attention to whether the question is asking you to round to tens, hundreds, thousands, or whatever.

solution—*n*. answer. As in "Pick the <u>solution</u> that would best solve Tim's dilemma." If Tim is in a batting slump, the best <u>solution</u> might be for Tim to take extra batting practice.

suggests—*v*. leads you to believe. As in "the information in the passage <u>suggests</u> . . . . " This just means the passage doesn't come right out and say something, it just hints at it. It's kind of like a "probably" question—you have to read the passage carefully and trust your understanding of it.

Test Instructions

Reading Carefully

As you know by now, being able to read things and understand what you read is very important to doing well on tests. The way tests figure out how well you understand things is by asking questions using these three "Reading Carefully" phrases. So it helps if you get used to answering questions that use these words, no matter what kind of reading it is.

My favorite things to read are, in order, the online *Los Angeles Times* sports page, *Sports Illustrated*'s pro surfing coverage, and the Harry Potter series. So as long as J. K. Rowling keeps pumping out books, the Dodgers keep playing baseball, and the waves keep coming in to shore, I am going to be reading for the rest of my life. You probably have some favorite reading materials, too. That's what we are going to use in this next exercise.

READING WHAT YOU LIKE EXERCISE
Open your favorite book, magazine, or newspaper, or go to your favorite website. Pick a passage or article that's about one to three pages long. If you use a website, print out the article. Read it carefully, using your pencil to circle important names and underline important sentences. Take your time, really "get into" the writing. When you are done reading, write three sentences that start with these words:

> The author's purpose in this article is . . . .
> According to this passage, the author thinks . . . .
> The main idea of this passage is . . . .

Do this with at least five different kinds of writing. If you like doing it, do it a lot. It takes, like, five extra minutes, and you'll end up remembering a ton more stuff about things you actually like.

WhizWords

best
probably
reasonable
suggests

Test Instructions

Probably

Not everything in life is absolutely, positively 100 percent obviously true. Come to think of it, almost nothing is. That means you have to get used to recognizing degrees of possibility.

For example, the Lakers are **probably** going to be really good for a long time because they have the best one-two punch in basketball: Kobe Bryant and Shaquille O'Neal. And it's **reasonable** to **suggest** that Britney Spears is going to be popular for a long time because she's so . . . talented.

What's my point? My point is that even if you don't know something is absolutely, positively 100 percent obviously true, you can still **probably** know a whole bunch of things. And on tests, one of the keys to doing well is being able to figure out what is **reasonable**, and what is not.

If you are having trouble on tests figuring out what is **probably** true, a good way to get some perspective on things is to think "What would Mr. **Reasonable** do?" And everyone knows who the most **reasonable** people on the planet are. Newscasters!

Related Word

approximate—v.
to come close
to; to estimate.
Math tests often
ask you to
approximate
something,
which means
using the
information
they give you to
get an answer in
a general range.

MR. REASONABLE EXERCISE

If you don't watch the nightly news already, take half an hour out of your busy schedule for a few nights and watch the Big Three: CBS (Dan Rather), NBC (Tom Brokaw), and ABC (Peter Jennings). Pick the newscaster who strikes you as the most reasonable of the bunch—the guy who would probably pick the right answer on a test. Mine is Tom Brokaw. He seems like he would make a good, reasonable guess.

Now get a pencil and paper. Write your guy's name on the top of a piece of paper. Now sit down with a parent or friend and watch the news! Have your news buddy write down four questions about news stories from the nightly news, using the four "Probably" words. For example:

What word best describes George W. Bush's face when a cell phone rang during his press conference? What is he probably going to do the next time a reporter's cell phone rings?

Before you answer, think "How would Tom Brokaw answer?" Do this every night for a week, and you'll probably get the hang of the "Probably" words and questions.

Hint: One way to be sure you've come up with the right answer to a question using a "Probably" word is to write a response that includes the word "because," *because* this will require you to go back to the reading passage to find information to prove your point. If you can't find evidence to back up your answer, you're probably wrong.

Chapter 6
All-Purpose Words

List the three classmates you collaborate with the most:

1. _____
2. _____
3. _____

inconvenient—adj. a lot of trouble.

● **adjacent**—*adj.* beside; next to. The sidebars in this book are adjacent to the Whiz Word definitions.

● **collaborate**—*v.* to work together. You learn best when you collaborate in the classroom. My science teacher has us collaborate on projects, but I've been having trouble getting anyone to work with me since I accidentally lit my lab partner's Skittles on fire with a Bunsen burner.

● **consistent**—*adj.* steady; always the same. The best way to do well on tests is to be consistent with your studying. Cramming for tests may work once in a while, but in the end you won't remember as much.

● **constructive**—*adj.* helpful. The word is most commonly used in the phrase "constructive criticism," which means you are doing something wrong, but the person telling you is only trying to help by pointing out your errors and showing you how to improve.

● **contradiction**—*n.* something that disagrees with something else. You have probably heard the phrase "a contradiction in terms." That's when two words in a row contradict each other, like: "an easy test." Tests aren't usually easy. Tests often ask you to find contradictions in stories and passages. That is where two statements or pieces of information do not agree with each other.

● **convenient**—*adj.* easy; handy. This book is incredibly convenient to keep around. It's small, and it has tons of the words you need to know. Just put it in your bookbag and keep it there. Whenever you have a question about a word, this book will be conveniently in your bag and you can look it up.

● **conventional**—*adj.* normal; accepted. One phrase that's used a lot is "conventional wisdom" as in: Conventional wisdom says that short people aren't that successful at basketball.

● **logical**—*adj.* reasonable; making sense. Logical is kind of the opposite of *emotional*. When you get emotional on tests, you can really mess up. Try to stay logical as much as you can, going from one question to the next without getting too worked up.

● **objective**—*adj.* fair; impartial. To remember this word, just think about what kind of opinions an "object" like a chair would have. Answer: no opinions, objects don't have opinions.

precise—*adj.* exact; accurate. Tests kind of go back and forth from asking you to be <u>precise</u> with your answers to asking you to estimate (make a reasonable guess). So make sure you pay attention to <u>precisely</u> what the test question asks for.

predict—*v.* to guess in advance. Some test questions ask you to <u>predict</u> what will happen in an experiment or in a story. That means you are supposed to look at the facts and make a logical conclusion as to what will happen. (See the definitions of *logical*.)

relevant—*adj.* related to the matter at hand. Sometimes on tests, you are asked to use only <u>relevant</u> information—that means information that matters (as opposed to stuff that does not matter). For example, if you are taking a test on making cheese, milk is <u>relevant</u>, because it's an ingredient in cheese, while information on fingernails is not <u>relevant</u> (it is <u>irrelevant</u>).

strategic—*adj.* planned. This word is used a lot when talking about war—especially about generals' "<u>strategic</u> maneuvers." Chess is a game that also requires a lot of "<u>strategic</u> maneuvers." Speaking of which, when you are taking tests, it can be important for you to have a <u>strategy</u> going in, like "I am going to stay cool no matter what" or "I am going to do the easy questions first and the hard ones second." Both of those are good <u>strategies</u>.

systematic—*adj.* acting according to an organized plan. <u>Systematic</u> is a lot like *strategic*—they both are used a lot when talking about a powerful person, like a general or dictator, who has a master plan and a strategy or a system to carry it out.

tangible—*adj.* touchable; real. This book is <u>tangible</u>—it is real and you can touch it. The word is used a lot in the phrase "<u>tangible</u> benefits," which means good things that actually happen. For example, my friend Kevin realized the <u>tangible</u> benefits from all his time in the kitchen when he won first prize in the cake baking contest.

Try to predict your grade on a test before you take it, then see how close you are to your prediction.

Antonym

irrelevant—**adj. not pertaining to the matter at hand.**

intangible—**adj. not touchable.**

All-Purpose Words

Celebrity Hot Tub

You can also do this with flash cards—write the word on one side, and the question using the word's definition on the other.

Did you ever want to be one of those reporters on *Entertainment Tonight* or *Extra* or *Inside Edition* who just spends all of his or her time running around, interviewing celebrities at parties? Or better yet, a VJ on MTV who just hangs out and chats with bands and singers who come by the show's studios? Well, I have.

My idea is that I'd have the celebrities over to my house and interview them sitting in my parents' hot tub. We'd relax in our bathing suits, sip lemonade, and talk about whatever they wanted to talk about. I'm actually thinking about doing this for my public access cable station or doing a webcast. I just haven't figured out how to arrange the microphones without all of us getting electrocuted.

CELEBRITY HOT TUB EXERCISE

For this exercise you are going to need a pad and pencil. Write down "Celebrity Hot Tub" at the top of a page. Now, go to one of the chapters and write down ten words that you are having trouble with. Just read through the words and definitions from one chapter and pick out ten words where you are still a little shaky. Here are ten I picked from History-Social Science:

compensation	pragmatist
controversy	qualifications
eligible	resolute
impose	subversive
insurgent	usurp

Now form a question that you would ask a celebrity who joined you for Celebrity Hot Tub. Use the definition as part of your question. For example, this is a question that I would ask supermodel/actress James King.

Q: Ms. King, are you a pragmatist about your acting career? By that I mean, are you realistic about the roles you are going to get?

After you have written questions using ten words from one chapter, go ahead and write questions with words from the other chapters, too. Keep these all in one place so you can go back and review them (or ask them, should you ever find James King sharing your hot tub).

All-Purpose Words
Word of the Day

You know those daily calendars that look like a block of Post-it Notes? You peel off a page every day and learn something new—every day. My favorite one is the *Far Side* cartoon-of-the-day calendar. I even have a bunch of my favorite *Far Side* calendar pages taped to the inside of my locker. My favorite one is "The Night of the Crash Test Dummies"—it has all these crash test dummies attacking some poor guy in his car.

Anyway, the cool thing about that calendar and others like it is that you get to see something new every day. And that's the best way to learn vocabulary words, by using them every day.

Related Word

consecutive—adj. occuring in order, one right after the other. For this exercise, you are going to be learning words consecutively, one right after the other.

VOCABULARY CALENDAR EXERCISE

Until I can convince my book's publisher to make a WordWhiz word-a-day calendar, you are going to have to make one for yourself! This exercise will take an afternoon, so wait until you have a few hours to kill—maybe when it's raining out or you are home sick from school—to get started.

You can make this calendar one of two ways:

> With a brick of Post-It Notes
> With some other "something-a-day" calendar

If you use Post-Its, first go through them and make them into a calendar, writing down the days and months left in this year. (Use a wall calendar as a guide.)

If you use another calendar, find one that has a lot of empty space where you can write down a word and its definition.

Now, there are about 600 words in this book. You need to choose the 365 words (or however many days are left on your calendar) that you need to learn the most. Now write each word and its definition on your calendar.

When you are done, put your calendar somewhere you will see it the first thing in the morning: by your bed, on the sink in the bathroom—wherever. Read the word-a-day aloud, repeat it and its definition three times, then put it in your pocket. Try to use that word as much as you can on its day.

Word Whiz

California Middle School

Answer Pages

Here are my answers to the Whiz Quizzes and Exercises. To find out how you did on quizzes and exercises that ask you to write essays, create calendars, and otherwise use your creativity, run your answer past an adult who can decide whether or not you have used the vocabulary words correctly.

English-Language Arts

Whiz Quizzes

page 8
Use an adjective or adverb to describe each of these words:

The pizza at lunch today was *unbelievably* chewy. It was like eating pizza-flavored gum.

My soccer team has *bright* green uniforms.

I go to a *small* school.

My mom had a *fabulous* shopping experience last week—she got four pairs of shoes for the price of one.

I play a lot of *physical* sports, like soccer and football.

Difficult tests make me concentrate even harder.

page 11
List three euphemisms you or your parents use:

If I don't get *Tomb Raider*

I'm going to lose it.

Grandpa Angeles is <u>a few cards short of a full deck</u>.

If the Dodgers lose again <u>I'm going to be ill</u>.

page 12
Identify the part of speech of the following words:

blonde—adj., n.
threaten—v.
fake—adj., n., v.
mambo—n., v.

<u>Note:</u> As you probably can tell by now, many words have meanings that have multiple parts of speech.

page 13
Write the following sentences using metaphors:

Pam is <u>greased lighting</u>.

James is <u>two French fries short of a Happy Meal</u>.

90

Fabio <u>vacuums up ice cream</u>
like there is no tomorrow.

page 14
Write down your favorite
(or least favorite) platitude:

Least favorite: Life is a bowl of cherries.

Write down the premise of
the last movie you saw:

There's Something About Mary
Everyone was in love with a girl named
Mary, but only one geeky guy was her
soulmate.

page 15
Write a one-sentence summary
of the last book you read:

The Old Man and the Sea
An old man hadn't caught any fish in
quite some time, then he caught the
biggest fish anyone had ever seen and had
to bring it in to shore all by himself.

History-
Social Science

Whiz Quizzes
page 20
Name three rules at school
you advocate:

You must raise your hand before
answering a question.

Maintaining a 3.0 GPA gets
you in unsupervised study hall.

No shirt, no shoes, no service.

page 28
List three things you once
thought were futile:

1. Getting Shaquille O'Neal and
   Kobe Bryant to play together.

2. Reaching a height of 5 feet tall.

3. Achieving the high score on
   Arctic Thunder.

page 29
Who was the first president
to be impeached?

President Andrew Johnson.

page 32
Go to *www.house.gov* and find a piece of
legislation Congress is working on now.

House Resolution 700 to the Airline
Passengers Bill of Rights, sponsored by
Rep. Bud Schuster.

page 33
Name your nemesis!

Skip Aloha, the best surfer in my age
group. Some day I will defeat him! But I
haven't yet.

page 34
Name your favorite team's opposition:

The Arizona Diamondbacks.

Answer Pages

page 39

Name a limitation you have
had to transcend in your life:

I was really impatient a few years ago
and got upset over unimportant things.
I have worked hard to be more patient
and mellow.

Exercises
page 41
Government

Country	Year	Government
England	1714	Monarchy
Texas	1836	Republic
United States	1897	Democracy
Germany	1935	Fascism
Jordan	1953	Monarchy
Cambodia	1976	Despotism
England	1979	Democracy

Math

Whiz Quizzes
page 47

Pick the next number in
these number patterns:

3, 6, 9, 12, <u>15</u>

–3, –1, 1, 3, <u>5</u>

3/4, 1 1/2, 2 1/4, <u>3</u>

page 48

Circle the integers.

1/2

.6

(6)

(–6)

(–2)

(0)

3.2

6.9

3/4

(17)

(–12)

(243)

–55/3

page 51

Please square these numbers:

$2^2 = 4$

$45^2 = 2,025$

$-3^2 = 9$

$-41^2 = 1,681$

$7^2 = 49$

$-6^2 = 36$

page 52

Solve the following problems
with the variables $x=2$ and $y=3$:

$2x = 2(2) = 4$

$4y = 4(3) = 12$

$-5y = -5(3) = -15$

$x - y = 2 - 3 = -1$

$2y + 7x = 2(3) + 7(2) = 6 + 14 = 20$

$-2x - 4y = -2(2) - 4(3) = -4 - 12 = -16$

Exercises
Circles
page 55

Quarter	$d = 2(1 \text{ in}) = 2 \text{ in}$
	$c = 2\pi (1 \text{ in}) = 2\pi \text{ in}$
CD	$d = 2(7 \text{ cm}) = 14 \text{ cm}$
	$c = 2\pi (7 \text{ cm}) = 14\pi \text{ cm}$
Tire	$d = 2(12 \text{ in}) = 24 \text{ in}$
	$c = 2\pi (12 \text{ in}) = 24\pi \text{ in}$

Number Types
page 56

$.79
positive number, rational number

.327
positive number, rational number

2 1/2
positive number, rational number

4
integer, positive number,
rational number, whole number

–12
integer, negative number, rational number,
whole number

6π
irrational number, positive number

Number Relationships
page 57

	Mean	Median	Mode
English	85.71	92	92
Math	85.43	82	78
Science	94.43	94	94
Social Science	83.86	84	84
O'Neill	.291	.285	.256
Ramirez	.313	.309	none
Rodriguez	.300	.305	none
Jeter	.323	.324	none
Gwynn	.336	.329	.317

Science

Whiz Quizzes
page 62
Name five organisms that are part of an ecosystem at or near your home.

1. Koi fish
2. cat
3. front lawn
4. evergreen trees
5. ants

page 63
Name three more extinct animals or species.

1. Dodo bird
2. Tasmanian tiger wolf
3. Sea cow

page 64
Think of a name for your generation that is better than Generation I.

My pick: Generation Amazin'

page 65
Identify the rock's type:

Basalt—igneous
Granite—igneous
Limestone—sedimentary
Marble—metamorphic

page 65
What's another kind of insulation?

My sleeping bag insulates me when I camp out.

Which is longer?

100 feet of string
2,000 miles of highway
350-meter running track
Small intestine

List three things that are lethal to humans:

1. Some kinds of cancer
2. Power lines
3. Extreme hot or cold

page 67
Name a genetic mutation that helped this species survive:

Giraffe—long neck
Human—opposable thumbs
Elephant—big tusks
Cheetah— extreme speed

page 71
What kinds of sustainable crops are produced in your part of the state?

Corn and soybeans.

Nature is full of transformations. Name three:

1. Caterpillars transform into butterflies.
2. Ice transforms into water (and vice versa).
3. Seeds transform into flowers.

Answer Pages

Exercises

The Body
pages 73–75

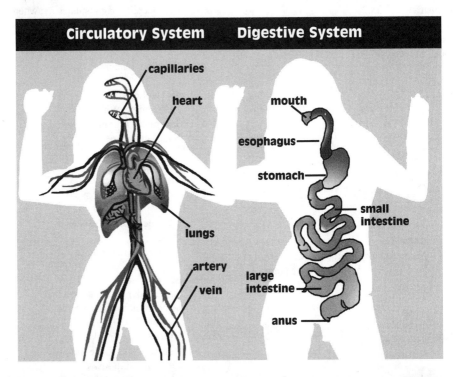

Circulatory System

- capillaries
- heart
- lungs
- artery
- vein

Digestive System

- mouth
- esophagus
- stomach
- small intestine
- large intestine
- anus

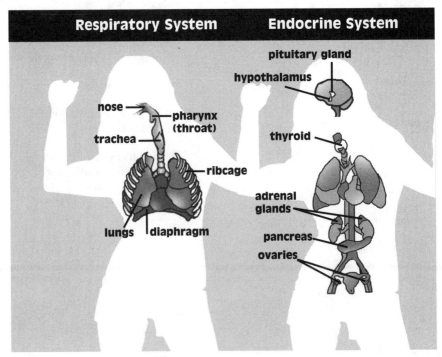

Respiratory System

- nose
- pharynx (throat)
- trachea
- ribcage
- lungs
- diaphragm

Endocrine System

- pituitary gland
- hypothalamus
- thyroid
- adrenal glands
- pancreas
- ovaries

Test Instructions

Whiz Quizzes

page 80

Circle your answers to the following "best" questions:

Man
Better
California

page 82

Circle the facts and underline the opinions.

The Dodgers hit 211 home runs in 2000.

They are going to do better this year.

The Dodgers beat the Athletics when they met in the World Series in 1988.

The Dodgers will beat the Athletics the next time they meet.

All-Purpose Words

Whiz Quizzes

page 86

List the three classmates you collaborate with most:

Frank
Judy
Mookie

Also Available